THE VALUE OF EDUCATIONAL PARTNERSHIPS WORLDWIDE WITH THE ARTS, SCIENCE, BUSINESS, AND COMMUNITY ORGANIZATIONS

M. Helen Mitchell

THE VALUE OF EDUCATIONAL PARTNERSHIPS WORLDWIDE WITH THE ARTS, SCIENCE, BUSINESS, AND COMMUNITY ORGANIZATIONS

Samuel Mitchell

REVISED EDITION

Mellen Studies in Education
Volume 87

The Edwin Mellen Press
Lewiston•Queenston•Lampeter

Library of Congress Cataloging-in-Publication Data

Mitchell, Samuel, 1936-
   The value of educational partnerships worldwide with the arts, science, business, and community organizations / Samuel Mitchell.
      p. cm. -- (Mellen studies in education ; v. 87)
   Includes bibliographical references (p.) and index.
   ISBN 0-7734-6631-2 (hc)
   1. Education, Cooperative. 2. Community and school. 3. Industry and education. I. Title. II. Series.

LC1049.M58 2003
371.19--dc22

                                                                          2003059674

This is volume 87 in the continuing series
Mellen Studies in Education
Volume 87 ISBN 0-7734-6631-2
MSE Series ISBN 0-88946-935-0

A CIP catalog record for this book is available from the British Library

Front cover collage by Patricia Leahy

       The Edwin Mellen Press   The Edwin Mellen Press
              Box 450   Box 67
         Lewiston, New York   Queenston, Ontario
         USA 14092-0450   CANADA L0S 1L0

              The Edwin Mellen Press, Ltd.
              Lampeter, Ceredigion, Wales
              UNITED KINGDOM SA48 8LT

         Printed in the United States of America

Dedication

Many professional women have supported the research that this text brings together. This book is dedicated to Helen Mitchell, Patricia Klinck, Diana Lauber, Yvonne Hebert, Aimee Horton, Ann Groves, Cathy Littlejohn-King, and Sheila Miller. Professional partnerships would be impossible without the work of such active women. Partnerships remain vital only as long as they integrate gender with other perspectives. My work on partnerships would not have been possible without these and other women who prefer to remain anonymous.

TABLE OF CONTENTS

Acknowledgments

The major contributor to this book is my wife Helen Mitchell who has drawn on her teaching experience to edit this book. Helen has contributed a line drawing which she has given her permission to reproduce. The book draws on six previous books dealing with change and partnerships that are based on many original sources (Mitchell, 1990; Mitchell, 1995; Mitchell, 1996; Mitchell, 1998; Mitchell, 2000a; and Mitchell, 2002). In order to limit the citations, the bibliographies of these previous works are cited unless a quote, quantified result, or specific point is involved from the original writings. The interviews and personal visits are cited in each case; the contribution of the large number of people involved as been invaluable.

Although their publications are cited, this work has received the help and assistance of the Copenhagen Centre. Their work on European companies and community groups has been an inspiration. The assistance of their director and staff is appreciated. A number of former students and current graduate students contributed to this book. Rob Evans and Diana Lauber have both commented on the work and attempted to introduce it to a wider audience. Catherine King, Marie Farrell, Jennifer Lock, and Teri Oberlin helped edit the work. Many other friends and students have contributed to the on-going work on partnerships. Paul Molyneux made the photograph that is used with his permission for the cover of this book. Patricia Klinck has given permission for her "Afterword" from the collection *Worldwide Partnerships for Schools with Voluntary Organizations, Foundations, Universities, Companies, and Community Councils* to be quoted at length as it is in Chapter 6.

Foreword

The significance of partnerships is underestimated because financial support is thought to be their main contribution. Classes are positively affected by many partners who represent a cross-section of society. Businesses are most publicized, yet represent a minority of partnerships. Individuals are the most frequent partners while groups include service clubs, the arts, foundations, universities, and businesses (Calgary Board of Education, 2003). Schools are being transformed by partnerships because they involve a great many volunteers; organizations of volunteers promote the further expansion of partnerships.

From the many different contributors, partnerships are able to bring a variety of perspectives together in schools. The larger community is no longer 'others.' As they learn from community members, students view education differently. For example, as executives are seen writing business letters and appreciating literature, this will affect the willingness of students to write. In order to bring varied perspectives to schools, individuals must see alternatives to established ways. The perception of alternatives allows people to go beyond the answers permitted by those with power

Partnerships are part of a search for changes in policies and programs in education and society. Partnerships create alternatives on the borders where they can influence both internal and external changes. People on the boundaries of organizations see the way other groups differ from their own employers. Partnerships open up an organization to challenges posed by those who are not a part of the usual decision-making procedures. Partnerships may become mechanisms of altering policies and programs in education and society on a continuing basis, much like a separate order in the church that challenges the regular institution.

Changes are possible only if individuals feel they are compatible with the organization; such innovators seek to avoid being restricted by preexisting status positions or stereotypes associated with them. These individuals find alternatives through their perception of contradictions and differences among cultural groups to which they belong. Exceptional individuals will be supported by organizations that make continuing innovations an important part of their vision.

An integration between different types of individuals is necessary for partnerships to develop. The variety of partnerships requires continuing review of school policies. When huge numbers of partners work with schools, a federal system of coordinating partnerships is necessary. Systems of partnerships must also relate to their constituents. Marginal individuals give the organization an open quality in order to make innovation possible. Like trading arrangements and markets, the marginal person provides the means for exchanges between organizations and cultures. Such individuals are a part of both worlds, but are absorbed by neither system. The irony of partnerships is they make individuals more important than ordinary organizations.

Creativity is an important goals for community members, educators, and, most of all, students. Each member of the partnership is a link in realizing a common aim. The inclusion of a greater number of community members means that partnerships make society more democratic. Partners can lessen the division between those who have resources and those who lack them; they provide for an expansion of social consciousness by increasing the sharing of power. Those in the more powerful positions may learn that real power is the ability to empower others. Therein lies the true worth of partnerships.

PREFACE

The Value of Educational Partnerships Worldwide with the Arts, Science, Business, and Community Organizations brings to the forefront the complex and rich relationships between schools and partner organizations. Dr. Mitchell's framework for looking at partnerships and the international context he brings to this work provides needed critical attention to these essential relationships.

Partnerships to help "at risk" children and their families abound in many large, urban public school districts in the United States. Some are coordinated; most are not. Many partners that work with low-income or minority children and families see the schools as rich cultural communities and utilize the assets of the communities through reciprocal interactions. Others focus on what is purported to be missing in peoples' lives, using a deficit model of partnering. Some organizations work to provide support and enrichment that districts no longer provide or perhaps never did. Parents are important partners whose roles range from making sure that their children do their homework to going on school field trips to becoming full partners through governance councils that have considerable authority over school spending, education plans and principal selection.

Partnerships, as described in the book, are experiments. New experiments in mayoral takeovers have brought about whole new partnerships between city agencies and schools that can be mutually beneficial, at least politically. Trends in foundation giving promote collaboration between organizations supporting schools and these foundations funnel resources to organizations, rather than granting funds directly to school districts.

This book provokes important new thinking and much needed discussion about the types and functions of partnerships and their effects on schools, on the organizations themselves and on communities. Perhaps, as Dr. Mitchell suggests, the division between public and private efforts in education may not only be redrawn in the future but possibly eliminated--creating the reality of a whole village raising our children rather than an over-used slogan.

Diana Lauber

Managing Director

Cross City Campaign for Urban School Reform

Chapter 1
Introduction

. . . partnerships will be the single most important governance
innovation in the coming years (Zadek, Hojensgard & Raymond,
2001, p. 26)

References to partnerships are currently common in our society. It is one step beyond
action by separated organizations and isolated individuals. Partnerships are often
seen as requiring a series of planned procedures, such as a needs survey or a brief
statement, to be approved by the partners. Other partnerships are undertaken because
individuals want to work together on a new approach or philosophy (Mitchell, 2002).
Neither specific procedures nor a vision statement is enough to create partnerships
that contribute to education. To alter school practices, these collaborations must
lead to new relationships within schools and between schools and their communities.
They must do more than develop rational plans.

RATIONALE

Partnerships for schools respond to different demands. Among developed
countries, different emphases are given to partnerships (Mitchell, 2001b). In North
America, business partnerships, which is what is commonly associated with the term,
are sought to support schools because governments are providing less and less
financial funding for education. Partnerships are so dominated by those run by
businesses that most educators fail to see the variety among potential partners and the
many different contributions that they can make to schools. Business partnerships
may bring a way of looking at education that is stereotyped. The bottom line may not
equal educational excellence. The literature on effective partnerships reflects a
singular contribution of one partner to effectiveness. The term "sustainability" is
invented and reinvented by many different authors (Mitchell, et al., 2004).

Both abroad and at home, partnerships for schools respond to different demands. Shortages of arts teachers leads to artists aiding schools. Limited training of teachers in the sciences is a reason to create programs for scientists coming into schools. Political demands for student responsibility often are a justification for community service as a requirement for graduation. Improving student academic performance is an aim for most partnerships although better citizenship is also an important goal.

In Europe, organizations, such as the Copenhagen Centre, view partnerships as a way to reconstruct society and to achieve greater inclusion of racial, ethnic, gender, and special education groups (Zadek, Hojensgard & Raynar, 2001). A reconstruction of society through partnerships leads to a strategy for teachers to improve their classrooms by including minority students. Corporations are expected to become more responsible citizens as a part of the same movement.

Companies and other organizations are integrating minorities as a part of the emerging goal of social responsibility. In Australia, the Education Foundation acts as an intermediary between companies and schools. This foundation sees education as a source of social capital, involving ideas and people (Black, 2004). Companies work there with the Education Foundation to improve the environment and provide opportunities for students to act as leaders in their communities. Worldwide, alternatives to present perspectives are sought in other countries for students who are either not in schools or who are low achievers when attending them.

In America, if such ideas are to be more developed, higher education and research centers would need to raise the horizons of teachers. Teachers are too involved in immediate problems to search for alternatives by themselves. Although there are limits to their traditional thinking, university academics are able to develop ideas, publicize results, and legitimize the practice of partnerships. For example, students and teachers in a school criticized Shell Oil for its complicity in the death of a Nigerian poet. The company terminated its partnership in Calgary (Mitchell, 1998). Shell might expect criticism from university faculty or students, since universities have a long history of criticizing corporations, while public schools do not.

Partnerships are a means for adapting to changes in different ways. Personal lives are transformed when the individuals' self-concepts and spiritual concerns are affected. For those involved, times and occasions alter. Celebrations make these alternatives significant. Although they are not religious, leaders of partnerships experience conversions, similar to Saint Paul (Mitchell, 1990). Celebrations symbolize change for those not so completely involved in partnerships.

Changing and conflicting views about education create a demand to orchestrate the diversity among partners. Some partnerships involve a mutual change in expectations. Employers, parents, artists, and scientists may all come to see each other, as well as schools, differently. Councils of partners may emerge to avoid chaos among the growing variety of partnerships.

For each individual partnership there is the problem of adjusting to change. Living together as partners is as different from marriage as school partnership is from the usual bureaucratic way of organizing schools. In any given society, marriages are thought to be an established path with a set sequence, while the alternative arrangements are diverse, changing, and regularly reconsidered. Among young people in Canada under thirty and all other adults in Quebec (a province prone to cultural change), the majority of couples are living together (Foss, 2002). The independence of the parties involved is becoming more important than the continuity of the family.

In other ways, partnerships are more like living together than a marriage. Partnerships involve searching and exploring for a common agenda where there is no set expectation. If goals are numerous and complicated, and a mutual adjustment in expectations is involved, a partnership is the path to follow (Mitchell, 2000a). Partnerships may involve a mutual change in expectations. Organizations, such as clinics for small children and elementary schools, learn to share information and resources; they relate to each other, but remain independent.

Creative ideas, people power, and financial support are reasons for developing partnerships. Effective partnerships bring these different resources together.

Businesses and schools seek a common plan unless they are just adding resources to an existing program. More than money may be involved. Business for the Arts, which involves businesspeople supporting the arts, requires participation in the arts for anyone who wants to be an arts supporter (Mitchell, 2000a). Businesspeople and artists have a shared purpose when the businesspeople join the choir or prepare scenery while talking and working with the performing artists.

Partners with whom the schools are most used to communicating are parents. Parents are increasingly vocal about how schools should be run and what policies could guide their operation. Parents are changing because of changes in technology and conflicts within society. Due to information on the internet, partners are no longer dependent on authorities to provide them with information on schools (Mitchell, 1998). As a result of teacher strikes, some parents organize alternative positions to those of school boards. Other parents follow the publicized ratings of schools because they worry about their children's futures. Still, many parents accept the success stories about schools proclaimed by their administrators.

Parents want their children to have secure jobs and to become good people. Business innovators view schools as potential models of their own dreams about economic growth. Partnerships are open to many different kinds of contributions and ways of expressing them. In some cultural groups, parents contribute food for their children's classes when they do not feel comfortable in attending school meetings. Businesspeople may be so comfortable with their contributions to schools that they believe that their managerial approaches can be transferred directly to schools (Mitchell, 1998). Businesspeople, artists, or other spokespersons often become involved with schools first as parents.

However, the roles of people in schools become increasingly diverse. Artists offer teachers the opportunity to see teaching as an art; in turn, the schools may integrate the work of artists into the curriculum (Mitchell, 2000a). Retirees, including seniors who were teachers, bring the view of their past struggles that is similar to the contribution of Native elders (Mitchell, 1998). The challenge of diverse partnerships particularly affects multiple partnerships.

These changing and conflicting views about education create a demand to orchestrate diversity among partners. If different groups share a set of goals for education, there may have one uniform way of responding. Educators may then act as agents in place of parents to maximize their advantage, similar to a firm in a competitive market (Mitchell, 2000a). If this is the situation, the purpose of the schools becomes the same for teachers, parents, and other constituents. Bureaucratic schools and businesses are both based on such singular goals.

In contrast, partnerships relate to multiple realties in ways that muddy the issue of who is the agent or who is the client or customer. Partnerships cross these boundaries in order to adapt to change. Social services in schools provide an opportunity to meet a variety of student needs, although the professionals involved are often preoccupied with their own relationships or unable to change the core function of schools (Mitchell, 2002). Clients need to supplement professionals in order to speak for their own needs.

People working for partnerships may change their member organizations. They work for changes within by creating alternatives along the borders, thus altering established ways of acting. In Calgary, some women teachers retained a reporter who regularly monitored their progress in eliminating discrimination and reported to the chief executive (Mitchell, 1998). Partnerships are a part of a search for alternative policies and programs in education and society. Organizations may change to allow cultural diversity among members or alternative policies for groups (Shaw, 2002).

In Europe, there are three stages that public/private partnerships have undergone to provide social services (Shaw, 2002). In the 1980s, governments started exploring the provision of services by companies because jobs were created through the private sector and the private sector provided competition unavailable through central monopolies. In the 1990s, companies became more aware that they were accountable for their actions. These actions include social, economic, and environmental effects of their business plans – corporate responsibility. In the new century, companies are developing a strategy based on a greater recognition of both internal and external diversity. Gender, culture, and race require changes in the way corporations and other formal organizations act.

Diversity within organizations is confronted in various ways by partnerships in different contexts. In Europe, national conferences provide directions for partnerships to increase social equality; while in North America, local efforts take time to realize that they can reach similar conclusions by coordinating their varied efforts. American partnerships appear and disappear repeatedly because of the lack of experience with this form of organization. Europeans achieve greater continuity and then go on to measure the developments of partnerships. Underdeveloped countries are often pressured by donor countries to achieve greater equality, such as for girls (Rizvi and Sayee, 2004).

Abroad, partnerships evolve into a means of promoting cultural diversity by combining the efforts of public and private groups. Europeans overcome the public and private divide because they have a longer history in such partnerships. For over a century, social services were provided by private, non-governmental agencies together with the state. Vocational education is a long-tried effort by the state, unions, and companies (particularly engineering companies), which know how to train workers and realize the importance of doing so (Zadek, Hojensgard & Raynard, 2001). Countries in the South often link NGOs with governments because of the limits they confront and a history that does not separate public and private domains.

In North America, partnerships cannot continue without active participants. Partnerships appear and disappear repeatedly. These partnerships are often brief, some lasting less than three years (Mitchell, 2002). The changes reflect the variety of partners involved, but the rise and collapse of partnerships is dependent on the presence of key leaders (Mitchell, 1998). Partnerships require new and different people to be involved and to become a new source of leadership.

Most American businesses find education an unchartered area. As a result, educational partnerships are an experiment or a series of experiments. Businesses often lose interest in these trials after a period of time. Other community and non-governmental agencies develop relationships if schools are interested in them. Americans are drawing on one model for partnerships, churches, that they have long ignored. President Bush is trying to involve church groups in social welfare that are already an adjunct to school programs (Reid, 2002). Historically, the churches are the schools 'oldest partner;' churches operate schools and related programs that are supported by governments in many parts of the world. Religion can contribute to a sense of social purpose. After Hitler, vocational education in Germany included moral education.

The differences in vocational and technical education on the two sides of the Atlantic reveal how substantial the problem is of creating a sense of shared purpose for partnerships. In America, some exceptional vocational programs are protected by unions and have trained students for generations (Havighurst, 1964). In Europe, support for vocational training is widespread. Many European companies carry out extensive educational programs themselves, while only exceptional businesses in the United States do so. Even in America, German engineering companies have a greater sense of educational continuity and dedication to partnership than their American counterparts.

Worldwide partnerships are a pattern, called "fixed" or reoccurring ideas, for differeonnt institutions and societies (Kristensen, 2001). Our analogy of partnerships between couples is a part of this dominant pattern. There are unfortunate examples, such as Enron, using their business partners to hide their financial mismanagement, but everywhere people are finding partners. Aboriginal groups talk about their partnerships with band schools. Governmental leaders try them as an answer to problems in the underdeveloped continent of Africa (United States Agency, Office of Women in Development, n.d.). Universities seek a host of partnerships in other countries as well as other institutions within their own country. Many organizations are joining international organizations as affiliates (O'Connell, 1997).

Uncertainty about partnerships is revealed by the questions that are asked of them, but not asked of established institutions. No one asks if bureaucracies should go out of business, but participants may lose interest in partnerships, which then fall into disuse. Partnerships are expected to contribute immediately to goal achievements by participants, while older institutional ways continue, whether or not they realize their aims. Other organizations may continue while managers are doing the same things, but partnerships require leaders who reach for new goals. The loss of key leaders is devastating. Whether it is building houses or creating networks of schools with volunteers, the former American president, Jimmy Carter, has set a torrid pace. In the Atlanta project, President Carter brings together thousands of volunteers for at-risk families and children. Attempts to replicate his social activism falter without Carter or a comparable leadership group (Mitchell, 1996).

Similar to mentors, partnerships match people in the new approach. The participants need to realize their own ambitions and those of their organizations in the joint activities they initiate. Again, there is a parallel between marriages and living together. Like marriages, routinized ways of acting or teaching are supposed to be stable, predictable, and lasting. Partnerships are not a way of enduring forever, but they are a way of learning about changes and learning to be a part of them. Sometimes partnerships carry out research, but whether they do so or not, they find new alternatives.

New options may combine with existing structures. For example, artists augment the work of arts teachers and arts teachers may become coordinators for general teachers in integrating the arts across the curriculum (Mitchell, 2000a). Project coordinators in different fields may integrate their local efforts with national projects or international efforts, such as in science education. Partnerships are constantly spreading to many different groups. For example, a partnership between schools and the military for officer training in a high school, and the subsequent recruitment of former officers for the *Troops for Teachers* program, are related to a renewed interest in discipline and strong leadership (Dixon, 2002). These diverse efforts mean that partnerships lead to modest reforms rather than drastic revolutions in practices.

Partnership must reach far more constituents to be effective. There is only a small number of people involved with business partnerships, but that group is affected by them (Mitchell, 1998). Teachers who are not involved, are not impressed, while students are influenced to have higher morale, but not greater achievement on exams. Other partnerships may have similar results unless they affect the core activities. A broader base of activities is required. The Irish transformation, discussed in Chapter 4, is an example of partnerships that transform an entire society.

SURPRISES

There are a variety of promising partnerships in business, sciences, arts, and voluntary service. Chapter 2 examines these four options and the ways each group celebrates success. The growth of these separate partnerships increases the problem of coordination and the number of coordinators involved. More varied partnerships means more professionals are involved as partners as well as school specialists. Student connections to different types of partnerships assist all students, which they are more likely to do if they are coordinated. Schools that develop social reform aims are likely to help at-risk students as a result of partnerships.

Additional people and subsequent partnerships create attachments when professionals are helped by volunteers. It is important for volunteering to become a general expectation in schools and society. Long-established groups, such as the PTA, may change the direction of partnerships; newer, high-profile organizations, such as Communities in Schools, may develop partnerships with new supporters. Chapter 3 reveals that the leaders of these non-governmental organizations are often the catalysts who bring schools together with other partners.

Chapter 3 shows that either school or community leaders incorporate the different perspectives of many constituents. Diverse groups, such as students and retirees, join to develop strategies for difficult situations. The possibility of multiple partnerships emerges as the contrasting perspectives of different, sometimes antagonist, groups are brought together.

Accounts of leaders explain how collaborative leadership develops under different conditions. The educational leaders connect with student leaders through the efforts of a number of organizations. Expansion of partnerships can mean the integration of programs around student concerns. The opposite can occur when competition and conflict among partners and similar organizations narrows the scope of the formal partnership.

In cases where there is general cooperation, leaders are able to expand the range of partnership efforts. Visions of the future, when linked with the dream world of technology, lead to cooperative efforts. Relating different partnerships to stages in the development of children suggests ways in which many different partners for schools could create a common plan. A pooling of the contributors does not require their integration.

To either expand partnerships or integrate them, Chapter 4 shows that foundations are critical partners. In addition to funding, foundations bring in the experts from the universities in order to measure the results and legitimize the activities of partnerships. The partnerships may get people so intensely involved that reform becomes a social movement. Small groups of people may stimulate each other to look beyond the usual options. At-risk students may be provided with options that parallel the gangs to which they are attracted.

Chapter 4 also considers the challenge for leaders that linking local attempts in educational reform to broader movements for change involves. Social movements, including the environmentalist one, are related to art and multiculturalism (Larson, 1997). Partnerships may be extended into other countries. Globalization affects non-governmental groups as well as schools. However, local efforts may resist the international changes or select from them. Either internationally or at home, partnerships may expand beyond what they can control, and thus collapse.

The addition of churches may expand the depth and endurance of partnerships. Some church influences enter the reform movement as a result of social activities. Others are being promoted to reduce governmental expenditures and substitute voluntary donations for them. The conflicts that religion brings are feared, but religion may overcome the absence of emotion in education and the tendency of groups, such as artists, to neglect celebrations of success.

Aside from working with religious partners, broad partnerships emerge when the limitations of any one set of partners is recognized. It is possible for donors, such as foundations, to multiply the effect of their grants by having additional partners. New challenges replace old controversies. In Calgary, schools supported by private, charter, Catholic, and public boards work together in a health initiative. Partnership groups may themselves expand as they organize into two tiers or a council of programs for different schools.

Rather than expanding current efforts or relating existing organizations, partnerships may expand in new directions. Chapter 5 considers the evolution of partnerships involving the efforts of either creative individuals or innovative societies who create measurable and varied outcomes. The involvement of key individuals means the unchartered creative activities may disappear without those highly involved leaders. Group networks, including teachers, may lead to either widening perspectives or restricted visions. An entire society, such as Ireland, may align partnership activities with citizenship responsibilities.

People may be collecting information on partnership achievements and debating the results. Measurement does not have to be the province of experts whose results are ignored. Social indicators show the range of involvement for any or all partnership participants are more important than single achievement measures for students (Cobb & Rixford, 1998).

The significance of a few open organizations and leaders is assessed. A project that results from looking at outstanding efforts of key people is a basis for city planning by students. A teacher is unhappy with being named teacher-of-the-year and creates a center for recognizing a great many teachers. An economist reverses the usual practice and creates enriched activities for the weakest students. These are a few of the options considered and assessed in Chapter 5.

Chapter 5 relates changes in partnerships to those in society. Partnerships can expand to include a renewed basis for citizenship for most people. The division between public and private efforts in education may be redrawn if not eliminated. Minorities within the society may have their positions improved by efforts within schools as well as outside. In the case of one group of women, an advocacy group was formed within the system.

Women maintain most partnerships. Their commitment sustains voluntary efforts. Their style of leadership provides an alternative that emphasizes relationships with people. However, reform groups ignore their dependency on women and, at times, persecute them. The inclusion of other groups and the enhancement of their lives are goals for partnership, but participants must get outside the box in order to see these possibilities.

The perception of new alternatives is dependent on continuing the original conditions that made partnership possible as open organizations. It is along the boundaries of cultures and organizations that opportunities for innovations develop (Mitchell, 2000a). For example, innovations in Aboriginal partnerships are introduced by those who combine French and Native cultures (Cathy King, personal communication, August 24, 2002).

Individuals find that new alternatives are generated from their perception of contradictions and differences among the cultures and groups to which they belong. A degree of separation is necessary to achieve an integration of the conflicting experiences. Marginality can provide an open quality to an organization or a system that makes innovation possible, as opposed to a single status system (Carlson, 1965). Like trading arrangements and markets, the marginal person provides the means for exchanges between organizations and cultures.

CONTRADICTIONS

Marginal positions are the ironical link to the function of partnerships. Marginal positions find ways to weave between organizations which deliberately set out to realize a common aim. New combinations for partnerships come from those who are in between cultures and organizations. This in-between status is a basis for evaluating partnerships and extending thinking about them. Partnerships are defined by planners as:

People and organizations from some combination of public, business, and civil constituencies who engage in voluntary, mutually beneficial, innovative relationships and activities to address common social aims (Zadek, Hojensgard & Raymond, 2001, p. 25).

The unplanned results of marginality alter these deliberate actions.

The changing results of marginal people between institutions and societies is related to the problem of perception of benefits from partnerships. Although some people argue that benefits must be equal for the partners, most recognize that there is an inequality (Hiebert, 2004). Partners are seen as pursuing self-interests, but the lack of trust rather than the profits from the relationship appear to be critical (Ginsberg, et al., 2004). Leaders of partnerships are more involved than the actual ratio of cost to benefits would indicate; laggards are likely to exaggerate the costs of involvement (El Ansari, 2004). The relationship develops the benefits and minimizes the costs; celebrations of success, reinforce this position. Marginal people may be the only ones who are concerned with the real costs and the possible polarization of interests between institutions (Ginsberg, et al., 2004).

Partnerships provide an opportunity to develop a sense of mission that isolated teachers and separated schools usually lack (Mitchell, 2000b). Building reciprocal ties, such as between university students and those living in a poor community, is an immediate problem, while equality is a distant goal. Partnerships that focus on integrated services for at-risk students are most likely to become parts of social movement for reform (Black, 2004). Among a large number of factors that are linked to school/community relationships, less than a third involve partnerships. Although partnerships may be related to building capacity, so may many other activities. To list attributes such as vision, professional development, or curriculum requirements does not develop our understanding (Jacobsen & Gladstone, 2004).

The difficulties of combining utilitarian and social functions of partnerships have meant that the results of evaluating partnerships could be applied to the evaluation of any other human activity. Higher education partnerships must be sustainable, viewed positively by partners, generate positive outcomes, create open communication, and improve ways of achieving common purposes (Ginsburg, et al., 2004). What are the common purposes? Why should they be sustainable? If partnership has achieved its purposes should it not fold its tent and disappear? How can leaders achieve these many good results? Could leadership develop local concerns that become broader and international?

Multiple meanings for partnership are sought by examining the different contributions that each partner may make. Cultural and political boundaries affect the forms of partnerships. Individual partners are brought in as a result of separate roles, which is why understanding the purpose of multiple partnerships is so critical. Leaders articulate the goals of people and generate new opportunities for them by finding a whole activity that is greater than the sum of its parts. Social movements are the guide for what partnerships may become, not what they always are today; they build trust and capacities of people involved in their missions. Options for the future are permutations of possibilities from the present; developing relationships makes possible new and different results from partnerships for people.

Our aim is to avoid singular definitions of partnerships and limited measures of their successes. This chapter and Chapter 3 explore the various ways that partnerships are developed by different representatives of the community within schools. Chapter 5 and 6 focus on cultural and policy alternatives among partnerships. Chapter 4 is about social movements; it links these broad concerns. In each approach, the aim is to avoid the sterility of seeking simple definitions that partnerships might follow. Multiple meanings will allowus in Chapter 5 to map the future that these new forms of cooperation make possible.

Chapter 2
Four Types of Partnerships

Among school partners, business partnerships are the best known of the newcomers; they support schools, seek results from them, and celebrate their joint efforts. Scientists and artists bring their knowledge and perspectives into classrooms while students and teachers enter into communities as a part of service projects. Business, arts, science, and community service are like the four fingers of a hand, on which parents are the thumb that work, together to support schools. The hand image suggests a final vision of learning with financial support, varied expertise, and community direction. As will be shown, at-risk or other marginal students benefit from any of these partnerships, particularly if they are directed towards them.

Other allies involved with schools for common goals include parents as well as other professionals. Parents as a continuing support for partnerships are discussed in Chapter 3 (Lightfoot, 1978). Partnerships with architects, lawyers, military personnel, and police officers are discussed less often, while ties with churches were ignored until recently (Mitchell, 1996; Mitchell, 2002). These other professionals supplement the knowledge available to schools and provide purpose and leadership that will be discussed later.

FOUR TYPES

The four types of partners selected here suggest the options available to schools. Each group develops different types of relationships with schools. Business ties are built from organizational links among corresponding executives, while the concerns of parents are the education of their own children. Most professions operate through their respective umbrella organizations. However, a large number of science partnerships are, in fact, individual projects undertaken by scientists and technicians. The arts community brings a variety of individual and group contributions.

Community service calls on individuals to make a contribution, but a vast array of involved organizations make this possible. The term partnerships should not obscure the critical contribution of individuals as representatives of each type in schools.

Business

Schools seek financial support, in lieu of government grants. Critics argue that businesses make such donations to avoid paying higher taxes (Mitchell, 1996). However, partners with different motives can work together and combinations of motives can make the partners better problem solvers. Multiple partnerships expand the attractiveness of education for those students not reached by conventional efforts. Partnerships for have-not students connect them with schools and make their education personally meaningful as they receive support from adults outside of schools.

Enviroworks in Kingston, Canada, is a program that began as a way of substituting for reduced government grants, but developed to include improving the environment as a goal (Lamb, 2002). The program operates a warehouse from which students recycle construction material that would otherwise be abandoned. At-risk students learn skills in working with these materials. Related promotional efforts of companies and community groups provide opportunities for students to acquire a wide variety of skills, including market research.

Enviroworks goes beyond mere financial support, having discovered that companies want to be involved as mentors and advisors. The executives are interested in the work of students. Students go beyond salvaging materials through simple skills; they conduct market research within partner companies, and become entrepreneurs within other firms. Businesspeople act as mentors and evaluators; they like being contributors to education, rather than being asked repeatedly to support schools.

Enviroworks develops business thinking by measuring results. Classroom attendance increases; former students are likely to be employed; over 70 tons of construction and demolition waste is diverted from the landfill; over $1 million in additional funding is brought to the school board; the number of business partners in the program grows twenty-fold; and Kingston residents change their disposal habits. Las Vegas presents an entirely different set of problems for schools than their business partners in Kingston (Cavanagh, 2002). The rapid growth and high paying jobs draw both teachers and students away from schools. Prospective teachers are met with advertisements when passing through the airport. Increasing numbers of students, particularly Latinos, are attracted by the opportunities for their families and themselves. Dropouts among students are one of the highest in the country, and the turnover numbers for teachers mean that replacements for those leaving are always being sought.

A program of work and education, known as PAL or Prevention in Las Vegas, is attractive to faculty and students (Faulstick, 2002). A large number of teachers apply for the program that features small classes and common themes. In their junior year, over 300 students apply for the program, which has no minimum grade point average. Students are able to work in a job that has a future. One student prepares T-Rex effects for a company that makes robotic animals for parks, casinos and movies (Cavanaugh, 2002). Another student who was pregnant in her senior year is supported by other students; she continues in school to graduate.

Administrators and teachers support students involved with PAL. As a result of fund raising, students in PAL attend a Shakespeare festival and camp at a national park. A grant for $20,000 from the district for equipment in the first year initiated this program. In addition, the school devotes a part of its annual budget to support PAL. Teachers believe this program could be generalized for the whole school and replicated in other places. The new principal is as enthusiastic as was the retiring one who started the program.

Outside North America there are many examples of enterprising business partnerships. Because of its vocational and technical partnerships in many schools, Australia provides examples of how these programs lead to the survival of remote communities (Kilpatrick, et al., 2002). Developing fish farms, new crops, or animals allows schools to develop certificate programs. Small businesses and trades are encouraged as future occupations for students. Partnerships become a catalyst for community development that brings knowledge and resources together. The schools in these partnerships develop leadership. In a rural community the same people are frequently called upon to implement new plans; student leaders provide an alternative. The new initiatives in Australia encourage young people who are not successful in academic programs to develop their skills in other areas (Black, 2004). As a result of such opportunities, at-risk students become leaders.

Arts

The different arts can be a basis for community action and a means to connect with anti-school groups (Mitchell, 2000a). In the Canadian city of Kingston, the symphonic partnership supports the teaching of music, while following the curriculum in grade 4. The school boards, the symphony, and the university's school of music create a grass-roots program which reaches into the surrounding communities. The Kingston Symphony performs a concert as part of the curriculum, while grade 4 students participate in the concert by performing with the symphony. Music becomes a powerful basis for community organizing. This program is especially important when many students psychologically withdraw from schools.

The above program is similar to many other partnerships where artists transform education. The Lincoln Center in New York supports a program of jazz music with over 100 musicians entering the schools in Memphis. In one planning session for the Memphis Arts Council, two artists were acting out the roles of artist and teacher; the artist turns and says: "You are leaving, I am leaving too" (January 22, 1998). The role play dramatized the tendency of teachers to abandon their classrooms to artists, when these substitutes appear to cover what the teacher thinks is a class subject. The teachers and artists need to be interested in learning to work together if students are to be motivated.

Cooperation is essential for any partnership that aims to become a part of education. In Rochester, New York, a plan involving a music partnership with the Rochester Eastman School String Partnership (RESP) gave students and community members an opportunity to enhance their musical knowledge and skills (Robinson, 1998). The private school, founded by the Kodak company and the city's school system combine to rescue music education from a series of budget cuts.

The students' group instruction at the public school supplements individual instruction, provided by specialists from the Eastman school. Senior undergraduate mentors select students and pair them with volunteers to encourage practice. The volunteers are rewarded with use of the instruments and training by students from the music school. A String Parent Group is designed to support the parents of the students in the joint program. The partnership lead to a growing number of students, as well as community and school members, forming networks.

Such networks are a part of increased opportunities in the community. Choral music is offered for those interested (Mitchell, 2000a). An integrated arts project with the assistance of several universities creates additional opportunities. Music education is provided for different groups: early childhood, older adults, and students from lower-income neighbourhoods. At-risk students benefit from participation in art forms as well as music. In an arts based school near Vancouver, students work together for the institution's goals. Students who rebel against the school's authority may achieve success in the arts and be accepted by their peers (Mitchell, 2000a). However, if students from these social and racial groups succeed academically, they are often rejected by their peers.

The groups for at-risk students often create a separate expressive world from that of schools (Mitchell, 1998). Through integration of the arts, schools support students' desire to express themselves and to become involved with others while maintaining achievement standards. A Canadian case study found that when a public school integrates student experiences around art, separate adolescent groups and cultures do not develop. As a result, exclusive cliques that divide groups of students are avoided (Gaskell, et al., 1995).

Unless recognition is given to their arts, at-risk students react against those who restrict their freedom. The most striking example of racial experience and specific arts is the association of American Blacks and jazz (Mitchell 2000a). Afro-Americans are attached to soul music and spirituals as well as jazz; they particularly reject country music. American Blacks are likely to participate in group performances and unlikely to attend museums or literary readings.

When minorities claim their own artistic territory, their view of culture reveals their tendency to want the opposite of what the controlling authorities envisage. This tendency is strong among Blacks and Natives and appears to resemble the tendency of adolescents generally to relish breaking norms. The social life of delinquents reveals they want the opposite of what is expected of conforming students (Mitchell, 1995). The rebels perceive the hypocrisy of the current system and wish to reverse the usual social and moral order.

Deviant cultures among adolescents frequently stress success through trickery, immediate enjoyment, and exciting events. Hard work and the life of a 'nerd' are not for them, but music is a significant part of their lives (Eckert, 1989). Separate music, drama or art groups often receive less administrative support in schools than athletic groups. Athletic leaders, rather than those in the arts, are typically chosen to be ambassadors for schools (Mitchell, 1995; Mitchell, 1998).

The Music/Theatre Workshop in Chicago builds on the link between at-risk students and the arts. Musical theatre allows these students to express themselves through different forms of art. Individual teachers find that students respond to musical experiences close to their culture – poor Afro-Americans often respond to rap music. Students generally find that choreographed theatre allows expression in movement, visual arts, and music (Lorraine Kneier, personal communication June 24, 1999).

Issues that include drugs, violence, and pregnancy as well as feelings are a part of the Music/Theatre Workshop in Chicago (Mitchell, 2000a). The plays are generated from themes in student lives. One play deals with a student who wins a football scholarship to Notre Dame while his father, discouraged by his own failure, makes fun of his son's ambitions The students write the plays with professional help from the workshop director, Meade Palidofsky.

In 1986, Miss Palidofsky began taking plays into schools and community settings (Mitchell, 2000a). In 1990, the first anti-drug show *Captain Clean,* was produced. Other plays followed, including *Someone You Can Trust* (about gangs), *Happy Birthday to You* (concerning teen pregnancy), and, *Temporary Lockdown* (involving jail). These plays are particularly meaningful to incarcerated youths; several have asked to have their sentences prolonged to continue performing in the musicals.

The Chicago program strives for varied links with young people. In order to get greater involvement of different kinds of students, the choir, and cast are separated. *Someone You Can Trust* was performed at the Chicago Historical Society with music provided by the Youth in Action Choir and students from the University of Chicago Lab School. One play, *Temporary Lockdown IV & V*, has a gospel chorus of twenty, together with an equal number of actors. Starting in 1994, the *Temporary Lockdown* series began a direct effort to have students write and direct plays. A number of students asked to stay in the remand centre to finish this play.

In other plays, students begin to acquire the voice of the community. For the play, *Someone You Can Trust*, the trial of students involved in a gang shooting is made into an opportunity for youth and their families to coalesce in the jury's decisions. The events involve adult and child characters who reflect on life and drama. After seeing a play, students use techniques followed by drama students in presenting plays (Music/Theatre Workshop, 1994). This role reversal includes studying the play's plot and key words and the use of warm-ups, circle exercises to develop trust, and writing diaries. The diary involves sections of the play that is related to the students' own lives. Experiences and memories of particular people help the actor develop a character.

Discussions following the plays reveal that over ten percent of students are considering suicide (Meade Palidofsky, interview, May 15, 1996). Referrals are made to appropriate outside agencies for these troubled youths, but a specialist is on-call when each presentation occurs. In addition, a graduate student in psychology or counselling is available for debriefing (Ibid). Other programs are built around combinations of case workers and artists (Institute for Community Development and the Arts, 1996).

Research on the music theater in Chicago as well as elsewhere shows that these programs reduce juvenile delinquency (Institute for Community Development and the Arts, 1996). This research generates support for arts education which would not occur otherwise. For example, in Chicago the evaluation study was funded by a $386,000 grant from the federal government, and the Annenberg foundation provided support for the musical drama as part of the regular detention school.

Without grants, individual artists often bring their talents and abilities to see opportunities where others see only desolation (Kilpatrick, et al., 2002). An arts teacher in the small town of Cowell, Australia, painted empty shops and persuaded their owners to display the art work of students in their shops. She organized students to create a community mural and is now viewed as a community resource to make other projects better known.

Science

Grants for science partnerships are available from interested foundations and governmental agencies, such as the National Science Foundation. Individual scientists and technicians receive this support (Mitchell, 2002). Scientists, including a group of Nobel prize winners in Washington, D. C., are volunteering to help in the teaching of science education in schools (Mitchell, 1998).

The Triangle Coalition for Science and Technological Education develops the support of scientists into an elaborate program:

• an institute for professional development of teachers; speakers' bureaus;

• loans and donations of equipment, financial support; scholarships and fellowships;

• technical assistance--proposal writing, consulting, etc;

• curriculum assistance;

- program development;
- public awareness campaigns;
- legislative/policy advocacy;
- job placement;
- career guidance;
- clearinghouses, databases, and hotlines;
- projects for women and minorities;
- computer-based telecommunications networks;
- administrator training;
- development of elementary and secondary school science programs;
- school restructuring (Fowler, 1991, p. 29).

Other programs pick only a few activities (Science Alberta, 2002). Science Alberta uses travelling exhibits, networks of scientists, and festivals to support a basic science program. Teachers receive trunks with surprising treasures from the foundation. Science Alberta organizes eight networks of professional scientists for teachers in eight cities. Across wider areas, teachers and students are brought together in festivals. A new multiple partnership is being planned to further expand these programs.

An impressive solution to the problem of connecting high-risk students with future jobs in the professions involves building upon ties among scientists, schools, universities, and foundations. St. Xavier in New Orleans has, from its very origin, worked with Native American and Afro-American students (Thompson, 1999). Results from tutoring these students and connecting with similar programs in other schools show almost half the students in this program go to graduate schools in the areas of science and medicine.

The summer program for high school students prepares high-risk students for a program at St. Francis Xavier or other universities in the sciences. Early in their college programs, St. Xavier enables students to participate in a common research effort with faculty. There is also an effective counselling program, and a free exchange of ideas to increase self-respect among its students. The students know that they are competent because of opportunities to prove themselves provided by the university.

The John Macy Foundation followed St. Xavier's approach for a variety of high schools (Williams & August, 1994). The Macy Foundation works with rural areas as well as blighted urban communities (Weisman, 1990). This program builds on the additional support that parents provide. For example, parental help is crucial for Native American students who leave Arizona for higher education in New England. Similar to the common research project at St. Xavier, a neighbouring university provides the resources for an advanced level of work for those students whose teachers previously believed were incapable of such learning.

The Macy Foundation approach is generalized into Ventures in Education (VIE) (Bleich,1996). The President of VIE, Maxime Bleich, does not understand why other schools do not follow the Ventures approach when they were turning away as many as 6,000 applicants. The VIE foundation supports students in public schools. The direct support by the foundation ranges between $138 per student in a rural area to $1540 for each student in New York City. Other attempts to enrich students' experiences through university support are available, such as in a program to support foreign language teachers in rural areas. Neither VIE nor the other programs are recognized or replicated in other areas or subjects because they are not seen as part of institutional change by partners.

Community Service

When colleges and universities plan for specific communities, a structure for multiple partners is involved. George Washington University in the District of Columbia is an example of this (Mitchell, 2002). Schools and universities relate classroom instruction to the burgeoning field of community service. For both levels, there has been over a 3,600 per cent increase in the number of American students involved in service-learning (Shumer, 1999).

Crisis events accentuate the demand for service-learning. For example, after the terrorist attack of September 11th, students in White Knoll Middle School in South

Carolina started a fund-raising drive for a new fire engine for New York City (National Commission on Service-Learning, 2000). From a study of their history, they found that, after the Civil War, a fire company in New York City sent them an engine. The Civil War destroyed their city's engine, and the Northern city sent a peace offering to replace the one lost in the fighting. To return the gift to New York City, $354,000 was raised for a fire engine. Returning the gift became the focus for the school's curriculum. History, communications, art, and writing were organized around this project. Crises provide a focus for service-learning.

Without educators directing community service, politicians step in with their view of having schools solve community problems (National Commission on Civic Renewal, 1998). The Canadian province of Ontario is requiring 40 hours of community service by high school students, but this is a result of actions by the government, rather than educators (Government of Ontario, 2002). Educators favor community service because of their concern for people. Training in such service increases future teachers' concerns for social justice (Anderson, 1998).

When politicians establish programs, moral education is often the aim of community service. For example, Richard Daley, Mayor of Chicago, sees character training as the aim of required community service in his city. Chicago, like a growing number of cities, requires sixty hours of service by all high school students (Washburn & Martinez, 1997). While, in the view of politicians, students are becoming virtuous and are helping their communities, school service-learning is also offered because it is a cheap and easy program for schools to provide. Administrators report one third of the difficulties of implementation, in comparison to other forms of experiential learning (Shumer, 1999). Average students benefit from community service because it increases their sense of responsibility without detracting from their academic achievement.

There is no evidence that community service aids at-risk students in school. Because school-to-work programs are similar in arranging for placement of students in the community, some writers assume that at-risk students will benefit from either program (Brown, 1998). Most students taking community service are from academic routes in schools while college students who participate come from a social class higher than the people in the communities they serve (Shumer, 1999). The International Baccalaureate program requires community service by their students.

Community service for schools is a total effort at civic involvement; at-risk students require specific assistance. Service-learning assumes that understanding other people and organizations is sufficient motivation for students to learn. Career programs for at-risk students provide incentives so that education is no longer unpaid work. The difference between the social position of planners and at-risk students makes it questionable whether both are talking about the same process. Materials for service-learning do not bring in the world of specific student groups. There is no evidence of community service programs drawing on the arts of students or their culture as more than a fringe addition (National Commission on Service-Learning, 2000). Community organizations are not usually involved in setting policies for school programs although they are involved in university projects; if they were, more of the administrators' time would be required for service-learning (Shumer, 1999).

Many of the programs make arbitrary demands that match the individual goals of politicians. No requirement is more questionable than mandating voluntary work. Since Maryland first mandated service hours for high school graduation, the issue of mandatory service has been involved. Voluntary work that is required is a contradiction. Students join teachers who are required to volunteer for extracurricular activities. Ri ght-wing critics see mandatory volunteering as a rejection of American individualism (Epstein, 2002). For such critics the contribution of partnerships to individual identity needs to be uncovered.

Voluntary partnership programs at the college and university level provide accounts of a reciprocal program that benefits both individual university students and community members. Such ties were created in the declining community of Shaw, which adjoins the White House in Washington, D.C. George Washington (GW) University works with the community and a host of organizations to tutor children and assist adults (Mitchell, 2002).

Over 700 GW students volunteer to help the Shaw community. In 1993, because of the large number of students involved in community service and service-learning, these activities became a major in GW's Human Services Program (Pollack, 2002). This academic and social project was supported by the Corporation for National Service. Student leaders, under the guidance of site supervisors, plan a series of events to catch the interest of university students as an attraction to volunteer service.

In the Neighbors Project, student leaders play a crucial role. Each year, 14 student leaders are chosen on the basis of their previous voluntary service and their potential to motivate fellow students. The process of selecting the team is competitive and involves project staff and community organizers. Students leaders are chosen to ensure a variety of cultural and religious backgrounds. They come to understand the differences among themselves, and between themselves and other people in a tightly organized community.

A series of workshops on diversity leads student leaders to analyze the life experiences of other individuals. Although linked only by similar ages, strong relationships form between community parents and university students. University students cross cultural, class, and racial bridges to join with other youths in the community (M. Anderson, personal communication, 1998).

The leaders learn to discuss these and other sources of diversity with new or volunteer students. An initial two-week pre-service training builds comradeship among students, introduces the community, and provides skill training (Pollack, 2002). Community partners play a role in the training of the student leaders, leading sessions on the four core areas of the Neighbors Project: health, community development, education, and senior services. The leaders visit community organizations, take tours of Shaw and its adjacent neighbourhoods, and participate in community service projects. Student leaders, who are very involved, schedule major events to meet the needs of both the students and the community. Each summer, before student leaders organize volunteer efforts in the community, community partners learn the university's plans through a session with the project supervisors.

Because of term breaks and student travel, community leaders see volunteers as somewhat unpredictable. Most student volunteers participate for a semester or the entire school year, while others come on a one time or periodic basis. Typical student activities include: delivering groceries to senior citizens, gaining city approval to renovate a playground and the grounds of the library, dispensing medications at the clinic, tutoring students, and conducting a violence prevention program for grade six students (Pollack, 2002). Local groups involved in this project seek to improve preschool education, recognition given to Latinos, medical clinics, support for seniors, and a variety of tutoring efforts.

It is difficult to assess the effects of this program on understanding diversity, but it has resulted in improving the appearance of the community and meeting the immediate needs of its residents. The results of D.C.'s 2000 standardized testing of public school students indicate higher student achievements. A *Washington Post* article (Blum, 2000) attributes the rise in scores to the extracurricular work being done with students. One partner organization, For Love of Children, oversees after-school programs and finds improvement in the reading ability of students by between one and two grade levels.

In 1997, a study by the National Center for Educational Statistics, Student Participation in Community Service Activity, found that the most important factor in student service was whether schools arranged or offered such service (National Educational Goals Panel, 1997). This same study found that half of the students had some form of community service experience and almost all the students who were asked to volunteer did so. The major benefit of service is personal development. Bonding and character development occur when students make actual decisions. When at-risk students teach younger students, a striking change often occurs in the demeanour of the problem students (Alt & Medrich, 1994).

The personal meanings that students develop make nonsense of the required service for graduation. Although community service might develop familiarity with volunteering, it should be voluntary once some efforts are made. Volunteers rapidly exceed role expectations. They choose how they will help others, unlike employees who carry out a task (Brown, 1995). College students are more involved in community service than high school students because they make the choice. High school students find it difficult to fit service into a life dominated by the individual pursuit of "jobs, sports, and advanced academic courses" (Mezzacappa, 1997).

Students raised in families who help others, continue to contribute in spite of the view of their peers. Unexpectedly, students who are both volunteers and rebels against the school's status system help other students with multiple disabilities and, over time, come to bond with them (Murray-Seegart, 1985). Bonding between people and the development of networks among students and parents are direct results from volunteering (Brown, 1995).

Impersonal forces limit individual volunteering. Volunteers decrease their efforts during times of cutbacks because the social distance between themselves and those needing help increases (McGrory, 1997). Improvements in expenditures inspire volunteers to help as they look for signs of success. External projects and demands are needed to make service learning a part of the curriculum. In Philadelphia, a high school English teacher, Ellen Weiser, devised a "Community Stewardship program, in which her students take inventory of the open spaces in their neighbourhoods, design and plant tree nurseries and gardens, and remove graffiti" ((Mezzacappa, 1997). Students and teachers then reflect on inventories or other demands in order to relate steward activities to their education.

Schools have the potential to receive volunteers from the community as well as send students into the community. The joint effect of volunteers for school and community is an integration between school and community institutions that goes beyond expectations. When schools are dominated by other institutions, particularly business, there is reason for alarm, but many different contributors increase the scope for meaningful involvement for all constituents because no single party provides dominates.

CELEBRATIONS

Community service gets students involved by recognizing and rewarding their past efforts. The William T. Grant Foundation announced an annual award of $100,000 to be given to an outstanding partnership (Robert Blum & Amy Gawad, letter, July 30, 2002). All forms of partnerships celebrate past achievements to a certain extent. Such support is important in recruiting volunteers. For business partners the recognition of student achievement is part of the public relations function, which is one reason businesses remain involved. Professional recognition becomes more important for scientists and artists as they participate in partnerships.

Community Service

Until schools are partnered, they often limit recognition to assemblies within schools or meetings in the adjacent community. University programs show how celebrations may be extended. During the 1999-2000 school year, GW student leaders attracted new volunteers through a day sponsored by *USA Today* as part of "Volunteer Week," that donated gifts to volunteers and a free barbecue for all volunteers (Pollack, 2002). Children were trained in arts and crafts, including pumpkin painting and macaroni art. The week to celebrate volunteers included a 5-kilometer walk to raise money for the homeless, the decoration of a local school, and recognition of outstanding volunteers among the many different projects.

From its inception, the Neighbors Project was funded by the Corporation for National Service, the umbrella organization for AmeriCorps (Ibid). The Neighbors Project is also supported by the Cafritz Foundation, which makes a large number of social investments in the D.C. community. The grants supply funds for the salary of a Neighbors Project Coordinator, stipends for Neighbors Project leaders, funding for retreats, training, supplies, and recognition activities. GW supplies many in-kind resources. Various university departments, including athletics and recreation, catering, and the students' union, donate tickets to events, food, and space for children to visit the campus.

Through its own version of the Academy Awards, GW highlights the exceptional work of students during a formal affair that includes a reception and ceremony (Pollack, 2002). The Excellence in Student Life program also rewards students involved in campus life through student government, the yearbook, Greek life, and community service. Volunteer students believe that their academic life is more meaningful because of community services they help create.

Business Awards

The other four main types of partnerships also provide awards. Business awards are the most elaborate. In both the United States and Canada, the Conference Board tries to influence educational policy through a system of awards that recognizes all types of partnerships (Mitchell, 1996). The Conference Board of Canada includes 100 companies who are the largest employers and combines the companies with universities, schools, and community organizations in its conferences, research activities, and award programs.

The Conference Board of Canada controls the legitimacy of awards for partnerships because the more powerful business Canadian confederation, the Business Council on National Issues, does not attempt to influence education (Ted Mieszkalski, interview, August 24, 1994). This council is composed of the executives of the 25 largest corporations. The Business Roundtable in the U. S. has a long-term commitment to education and recognizes achievements.

The business confederation, with its select membership, effectively publicizes and recognizes partnerships through its awards. In the United States, an extensive program of awards, the Anderson medals, is given by the Business-Higher Education Forum. The Forum, an affiliated organization of the American Council on Education, is limited to one hundred members who are university presidents and chief executives of selected Fortune 500 companies (Mitchell, 1996). A similar Canadian forum provides two awards on behalf of two companies.

At both the local and international level, business organizations or interests determine the legitimacy of partnerships. In Kingston, Ontario, Enviroworks won awards from Greater Kingston Chamber of Commerce, the Ontario Waste

Minimization Award, and the Recycling Council of Ontario (Mitchell, 2002). At the national level, this program received an Honourable Mention Award in the Peter F. Drucker Canadian Non-Profit competition as well as an award in the Conference Board's "Broad Community Collaboration" category.

Business related programs also receive international recognition. Among entries from 13 countries, Enviroworks was best in the category of "Caring for the Community and the Environment" established by the Nova Corporation. The United Nations Global 500 Award recognizes Enviroworks contribution to the protection of the environment. The United Nations award was given by the Japanese Prime Minister and the Emperor and Empress of Japan.

Although the Las Vegas example has not received international recognition, a number of local and national news stories have publicized its results (Cavanaagh, 2002; Faulstick, 2002). PAL is cited in reports as a model program and it meets the standards set by the National Dropout Prevention Center. The program should win more awards as time passes. Many business partnerships are celebrated as a part of special days, particularly in Australia (Kilpatrick, et al., 2002). Rural business partnerships may involve publishing a local newspaper or providing the community with a lumber company when it has neither. Videos and pamphlets publicize the cases of rural schools trying to survive. For all business partnerships, the creation of videos is a typical part of the celebrations.

Recognizing the Arts

Awards and recognition for the arts are seldom given by businesses and only involve a few governments. Government on occasion sees the arts as a source of community empowerment. In conjunction with community renewal in one New England community, Lowell, Massachusetts, the arts are recognized as a part of separate ethnic celebrations (Larson, 1997). These separate celebrations are brought together for a community celebration. A cultural unity can occur which gives new life to a declining community (Mitchell, 2000a). Rural communities gain a focus when they develop the arts, such as theater, in which many members of the community are involved (Mitchell, 2000b).

An independent, grass-roots program in Kingston, Ontario struggles to get limited recognition (Lamb, 2002). The Kingston Symphony Educational Partnership is based on a convergence of music education and marketing to develop a new audience under the auspices of the university (Mitchell, 2002). The concerts that are based on the school curriculum provide university music students with an opportunity to teach preparatory and follow-up lessons. The regular grade 4 teachers enhance their professional development through prepared curriculum and a music workshop, which focuses on the symphony. In turn, the Kingston Symphony reaches an extended audience of elementary students and teachers.

This partnership differs from other similar symphony concert experiences or orchestra partnerships because elementary students prepare for performing with the symphony (Ibid). This performance may vary and include either singing, dancing, or composing. Grade 4 students know from the beginning of the six-week study unit that they will be performing with the symphony; this performance is a major goal and motivator. Festivals and performances are so important in the arts that instructional programs may be saved by threatening to cancel them (Stake, et al., 1991). An Australian mining community won national recognition for its music program, designed as part of its campaign to survive (Kilpatrick, et al., 2002).

Arts education programs are not usually recognized in festivals or celebrations of success. Music educators receive greater recognition than others, but these focus on students. For example, a talent contest sponsored by Oscar Mayer led to an award of $10,000 for the schools (National Association of Music Educators, n.d.). Teachers, administrators, or program developers are not given such recognition. The most important recognition for the Kingston Symphony Partnerships came when the city's only daily paper did one story (Lamb, 2002). Teachers, school board personnel, musicians, the music director, music professors, and students were interviewed. The reporter visited one of the schools and observed a lesson taught by the university students. Several photos accompanied the story.

In major centers of the arts, such as New York, recognition occurs. The Lincoln Center's many local programs converge on a national festival for high school groups. The annual Essentially Ellington High School Jazz Band Competition and Festival builds group interaction and enjoyment for both winners and losers. The related Jazz for Young People Concerts, with help from Scholastic Inc., led to the creation of a curriculum package. These lessons feature a video and lesson guides that takes students behind the scenes of a recording studio.

Both in Kingston and New York City, professional recognition is replacing community support, but specialized recognition is not where arts education occurs. The National Endowment of the Arts identifies principles for effective music programs. Their principles are based on the study of model programs, not grass-roots partnerships like Kingston (Mitchell, 2002). The writer, M. Robinson, who told the story of the Rochester partnership received the Reston prize which is jointly sponsored by National Association of Schools of Art and Design, National Association of Dance, National Association of Schools of Music, and National Association of Schools of Theatre (1998). Writing about successful or ideal programs is not the same as organizing projects in local communities.

The arts have relied on writing about academic effects of the arts, rather than celebrations of community efforts. According to one study, listening to a piano sonata can increase the spatial reasoning and mathematical abilities of students (Anderson, 1998). Reading and writing skills are both enhanced by exposure to drama and the visual arts (Mitchell, 2000a). Evidence of links between academic achievements and training in the arts is less influential than the rhetoric that results from the philosophy of multiple intelligence advocated by Howard Gardner. Having identified some of the forms of intelligence with the arts, opponents of the arts are left to oppose developing abilities to learn (Mitchell, 1998).

Schools benefit from community support of the arts only in exceptional situations. Small communities which attract many artists or back-to-the-land people are able to support efforts by schools that more heterogenous communities are not able to offer

(Kilpatrick, et al., 2002). At major holidays, the arts provide performances that are also community celebrations (Stake, et al., 1991). The importance of the arts is recognized when a country is placed under dictatorships. For example, in Chile, the artists were the first group imprisoned because they could attack the pompous military leaders (Mitchell, 2000a).

Science

Science education partnerships have far more support from government and business than does arts education. Intellectuals in universities are becoming primary partners and their support gives added emphasis to teachers at the elementary level to give more time and attention to teaching science (Mitchell, 1990). Involving scientists as partners is the direction chartered by the National Science Foundation. Ventures in Education is an unacknowledged forerunner in this field (Hoff, 2001). Previous efforts emphasized professional development of teachers, individual scientists, or technicians, but these teachers left the schools after training.

Business, government, and foundations support the stream of new efforts in science education. Grants of $3,000 to help prepare for the NSF grants are provided by the Exxon Mobil Foundation (Hoff, 2001). In the past, science educators were honoured by American presidents (Olson, 1984). Local festivals are being introduced to celebrate the success of efforts involving business, foundations, and universities to support schools. DaVinci Days is a local Oregon example (Corvallis School District, Oregon State University & Hewlett Packard, n.d.)

The effort to improve science education began with Sputnik, but has continued with diverse partners and local sites. The momentum to establish partnerships continues, as illustrated by the 1996 National Science Foundation (NSF) theme, *Dynamic partnerships: Seeding and Sustaining Education Reform.* NSF's interest in funding collaborative partnerships is intended to achieve lasting reform in education (L. S. Willimas, personal communication, December 13, 1995). National organizations, such as the Points of Light Foundation, coordinate efforts by businesses, universities, and non-profit agencies. Examples of funded programs are

Partnering for Elementary Environmental Science (PEES), and Sciencing with Watersheds, Environmental Education, and Partnerships (SWEEP) (Mitchell, 2002). Support for the next generation of science education programs by professional educators and their partners is assured as it has been for previous experiments.

The recent approach to developing a program for multiple partners in science education is similar to the Galileo Educational Network Association in the Western Canadian province of Alberta (Jacobsen & Gladstone, 2002). This project, which combines technology integration with progressive teaching, received the Industry Canada – CanConnect Award for business-education partnerships by the Conference Board of Canada. The award is sponsored by Royal Bank, Daimler Chrysler Canada, Human Resources Canada, and Industry Canada.

The Conference Board of Canada award is a culmination of the extensive support and recognition for this project. Aside from a large grant from the Department of Learning, strategic alliances are established with professional and business partners, including two law firms (Jacobsen & Gladstonel, 2002). This network provides opportunities for educators and school division leaders to move towards strategic goals in collaboration with business, universities, community, and government.

Partnering with a variety of organizations involved in high technology creates multiple resources. For the Galileo project, some organizations provide expert advice: the Universities of Calgary and Lethbridge, the Institute for Professional Development at the University of Alberta, and the Pacific Institute of Mathematical Sciences. Other partners provide financial contributions, such as Cavendish Investments (Ibid). Most partners provide both money and in-kind donations including Stellarton Energy Corporation, IKON Office Solutions, Shaw Communications, Alberta Science and Research Association, and IBM (Ibid). IBM combines both forms of donations with expertise. AxiaNetMedia is helping to develop an on-line professional development model for teachers in a worldwide service (Jacobsen & Gladstone, 2004).

Partnering with technology firms enhances the legitimacy of the specialists from the Galileo network to teach school staff about technology. Galileo's expert teachers help schools create an integration of learning, technology, and professional development (Jacobsen & Gladstone, 2004). Galileo seeks teachers willing to discover their concerns and abilities, relate technology to themselves as individuals, and extend technology to the whole curriculum. Teachers and the over ten partner schools make a three-year commitment to this project. Only teachers interested in technology and supportive of efforts to improve schools are accepted, since Galileo's experience showed they could not overcome basic hostility to modernizing schools.

IMPLICATIONS

Partners are not able to perform miracles for schools. Not in technology, science education, or the marginal area of arts education is it possible to revolutionize education. Business partnerships have greater resources and community service has a larger potential to mobilize people. All partnerships are ways of supplementing the efforts of teachers in schools. Schools rely on gifts and volunteers for the celebrations as they did for starting the partnerships.

Different Kinds of Contributions

Partnership links are relative to the power of those involved. Volunteering by community members, teachers or students occurs when there is a more equal relationship. The arts are the only institution less powerful than schools. All partners are capable of forming reciprocal relationships. Universities are not only receiving help, but volunteers are being provided to the community. A sense of common purpose can transform inequalities in a partnership. Scientists and artists are both volunteers and professionals. They feel they must help even if the compensation is less than private companies pay for scientists, or is irregular, when it is paid to artists.

Businesspeople become involved when they are following their professional and parental interests. The Galileo project allows scientists, geologists, and lawyers to mix their perspectives while maintaining an interest in schooling for their children or grandchildren. Business and scientific partnerships may coalesce, but arts partnerships have to search for other partners, such as those in therapy or drug prevention. The word "arts" is often replaced by "creative activities" because of the marginality of this field (Mitchell, 2002).

Although the specific plans need to be promoted, community service is an important aim for the public (Shumer, 1999). People want educational institutions to improve the character of students and contribute to the community. Universities, such as GW, show how it is possible to involve a large number of organizations in a partnership. Community service suffers in schools from a lack of purpose; it requires a community crisis, such as in New York City, in order for the curriculum to be related to community needs. Otherwise, community service will be similar to integrated social services, a place to park student or parent problems (Mitchell, 1996).

The other partners also require an educational purpose. When activities with business and community organizations are followed with class work or individual reflections, they become effective. Arts integration offers the potential of transforming the entire curriculum, but all partnerships should include this vision. School-to-work partnerships may relate the academic curriculum of all students to the practical world. Science education may be the foundation for preschool education and a modern or expert system of training (Jacobson, 2002). Unfortunately, partnerships may turn out to be the illusion of our age for those hopeful of seeking change in education.

Having been considered as an antidote to war at one time, community service is close to the heart of the desire of educational progressives for innovation (Mitchell, 1998). Political and educational conservatives prefer to avoid any form of partnership. Other ideological groups prefer mixtures, depending on their values. For example, though the arts may be progressive generally, discipline-based arts advocates want specific programs that support academic achievement (Mitchell, 2000a).

Partnership is a step away from rugged individualism and a move towards a postmodern position. Chapter 3 examines the advantages of multiple partners for partnerships; this chapter has dealt with different types of partnerships that need to be combined in order to overcome the limited perspectives of any one partner. The organization that controls the money will be dominant unless people are organized and ideas discussed. There are significant contrasts between organizations that contribute ideas, universities, and those involving people through community organizing. It is between these two polar positions that partnerships for schools can evolve.

Several creative syntheses are possible. Enviroworks shows how the business, environmentalist, and educational perspectives may merge. In this program, individual teachers develop efforts to prevent wastage; their recycling efforts can be supported by the school, government, and businesses (Kilpatrick, 2002). It is the link between environmental concern and curriculum change that is crucial for such partnerships to make a significant difference. The Galileo project changes its partners through its educational approach, but it has different partners contributing to its multiple approach. Similarly, Ventures in Education, once it is defined as a partnership, changes community, and educational views of students who are rising from poverty.

Ventures in Education shows how at-risk students may become competent and successful. Arts education reveals links between the arts concerns of anti-school students and school work. Business partnerships combine resources, finances, and leaders to reach difficult students as well as employment for such students in exchange for academic improvements (Mitchell, 1996). It is the dream of those possessing arts knowledge to be similarly sponsored by such businesspeople. In major educational reforms, business support is solicited to supplement efforts by parents and teachers with the aim of improving schools rather than choosing between schools. In Chicago, awards of up to $10,000 are given for school councils and individual teachers each year (Mitchell, 1996). Separate awards are also given to teachers, students, and local school councils.

The Target of At-Risk Students

Every partner type is limited, but each tries to reach difficult students. The *effectiveness* of projects in Kingston, Las Vegas, and Australia results from the convergence of different partners. The limitation on partnerships is the number of perspectives that can be reconciled (Mitchell, 1998; Mitchell, 2002). For teachers, the concern is the immediate world of the school, while, for music or other arts, it is current participation by students as preparation for future attendance at performances, as these students become adults. Businesspeople see students as prospective workers and consumers. Scientists think in terms of preparation and motivation of those who will enter their particular field.

It is possible to stretch these different viewpoints. Scientists, artists, or businesspeople should help teachers to see partnerships in terms of both the local problems and cosmopolitan concerns. Business recognizes the significance of ethnic diversity. Art educators link mathematics with music. Teachers combine their concerns as parents with professional views. The problems of unemployed youth call for immediate answers as well as long-term thinking.

The difficulties of youth finding work have increased pressure on the educational systems to find solutions with employers in a great many countries (Vickers, 1991). The meaning of education might be transformed by cooperative work for at-risk students. Most schools ignore employment as a source of learning (Lerman, 1996). Schooling is related to employment in a variety of ways. The competition with part-time work means that school becomes "unpaid work" for students (Hall & Carlton, 1977, p. 69). Parents believe that combining vocational and academic programs would be beneficial (Mitchell, 1998). In a study of 39 local partnerships, only 16 percent of senior high school students reported participating in a workplace activity (Olson, 1997). 88 percent of students who had jobs during high school found them on their own.

The relationships between business and schools are often questioned. Students and employers are linked through part-time jobs. Such jobs are a source of immediate income for growing adolescent needs, but the jobs have little long-term significance (Mitchell, 1998). Part-time jobs often mean that students work long hours, neglect their school work, and opt out of extracurricular activities. However, working while attending high school has a positive impact on career earnings. Though such work may prevent or delay graduation, the long-term impact on earnings is positive, particularly for at-risk students (Lerman, 1996).

At-risk students develop a negative syndrome that begins on entry into the school system. Such students disengage themselves from schooling early in elementary school and neither identify nor participate in their education in later stages (Lerman, 1996). At-risk students lose interest in school and confidence in themselves, although they blame teachers and other experts for their problems (Mitchell, 1998). By stimulating their interests, increasing resources, and providing rewards, most at-risk students will improve their performance and attitude. The Acceleration Project that enriches the curriculum for at-risk students is discussed in Chapter 5.

Evidence from Career Magnet Schools in New York City shows gains in self-confidence among many at-risk students. Other studies report higher achievement in general subjects for this same group. When programs include job placement, the disadvantage of poor students in accessing informal channels to jobs is reduced (Lerman, 1996). The programs provide adult peer groups to prevent negative youth groups from pulling students away from both work and education, and getting into trouble or prison.

For the employers, these programs change their perceptions about the abilities of young people. Employers often wait for young people to grow older as an indication of reliability; career-to-work programs drastically change this. Of all employers who participate in cooperative work programs, most agree that students are productive workers. A general group of employers report frustration with young people who lack "discipline as well as communication, numeracy, and literacy skills" (Lerman, 1996). The schools provide a reliable screening function for cooperating employers who want a greater number of such students.

Unlike programs with only one partner, community projects, such as in Chicago, support a diversity of approaches reflecting the community rather than a single interest. Programs receiving initial rewards included the use of the Socratic method in teaching, holding meetings in neighborhoods from which students are bused, and requiring school uniforms in order to prevent students from displaying gang symbols in school (Jan Hively, interview, November 15, 1993). Community awards are likely to emphasize future directions since they do not have one fixed plan or set of options. When limited steps towards a broad goal are celebrated, future efforts are encouraged. Community service offers opportunities for celebrating the successes of other partnerships as it develops networks among many potential allies. Business efforts often make recognition and awards for partnerships into an exercise in public relations. Business awards need to be personally meaningful for both those giving and receiving the awards if they are to be believed by a sceptical public. Artists and scientists provide authentic educational experiences that are less likely to be questioned. However, the community alone contains the variety of resources and perspectives from which effective partnerships may emerge. Students, teachers, and parents may realize themselves as participants in a continuing sense of community promoted and encouraged by the celebrations.

The four types of partnerships discussed in this chapter provide a wide variety from which partnerships can develop. Individual and group efforts are included to ensure that partnerships are more than a group phenomena; partnerships include individual people and should relate to a diverse population. The differences between partnerships, as they relate to levels of education, ranging from elementary school to university, are important; diverse types of partnerships should be related to the development of unique and separate students.

Partners stand to gain multiple abilities and approaches themselves. Businesses will be able to relate to differences among students who, when labor markets are tight, they must hire. Scientists and artists will gain in developing approaches to making themselves better understood by those outside their fields. In community service, the potential for reciprocal ties between students and diverse groups in the society can mean that students become involved in creating their own futures. Community service is the least developed, but most important of the partnerships discussed so far. Each type of partnership should be directed to future benefits from working with students, not just immediate returns. The partners and schools are examined in terms of looking ahead to new realities in Chapter 5.

Other partners that are not included in this chapter can involve more controls over students. The military are provided with opportunities to recruit in schools as a result political actions by the Bush administration (Dixon, 2002). Politicians can make the schools in a football, such as in the Illinois case, where the state Governor and the city mayor are fighting over who controls the schools. In less political schools, the role of policemen within schools raises questions about the relationship between the police and schools. The school's inability to maintain confidentiality of student records is a typical issue that integration of school services must deal with. However, schools, unlike social work and medicine, may have their basic goals challenged by an increase in controls over students. Learning presupposes some degree of individual freedom. If students are to become leaders in the community, they will need more freedom. The dominance of business as a partner may already make this development difficult. Schools will have to draw upon more independent professions and individuals in order to maintain opportunities for student leaers to act freely.

Chapter 3
Cooperation Among Leaders

If you want to train leaders you have to start early. If you want to keep kids out of prison you have to start early. But it isn't easily done. We have to conduct research, educate a wider public, and mobilize citizen allies. We have to persuade diverse groups to work together-schools, social agencies, the faith community, law enforcement, all levels of government . . . .– John Gardner (quoted in Kennedy Y. E. L. L. Project, 2002, p. 21)

Although partnerships are arrangements among organizations, they depend on the commitment of individual leaders. Partnerships have different combinations of competition and cooperation, depending on the community context. Volunteers bring a commitment and understanding that makes them essential for partnerships; professionals who participate in partnerships could emulate volunteers. Professionals who enter into partnerships need to understand each other, support each other, and share a common set of ideals (Jacobsen & Gladstone, 2004).

The difference between volunteers and professionals is similar to the contrast between school administrators and student leaders. Professionals may be able to adjust to difficult demands, such as limiting the scope of their mutual plan when the organizations compete with each other. Similarly, adult leaders are more likely to see opportunities for partnerships than are students. Volunteers and students usually see the options as either cooperating or leaving the school (Brown, 1995).

Plans for different situations are based on the visions of leaders. By stressing the contribution of constituents, leaders are able to empower others to achieve the goals of partnerships (Gardner, 1990). Schools have the task of reversing the role of status so that constituents or followers are recognized as primary. Educational leaders are able to empower students and to increase the number of student leaders. Student leaders can work together with community leaders as shown in Chapter 2. This chapter shows the potential for combining student, community, and education leaders and celebrating their successes.

Programs to mentor students require cooperation with other individuals and groups. The national organization promoting partnerships in education began by helping local groups recruit and train volunteers (National Association of Partners in Education, 2001). The development of partnerships links local volunteers with national organizations as well the reversal of roles between leaders and followers. National organizations with a focus on students may overcome many problems. Organizations of volunteers are often catalysts for multiple partnerships. The voluntary or non-profit organizations advocate for students, particularly when it is an organization of students. Community leaders are more effective than student leaders, but school leaders can influence those who are influential in the other two groups.

OPPORTUNITIES FOR STUDENT VOLUNTEERS

Engaging students is a measure of effective partnerships (Mitchell, 2002). Although over the years students have become involved in local committees and boards of education, an increasing number of students serve on state boards of education. Their inclusion is promoted by the National Association of State Boards of Education; there are now 13 states with 17 student members in the United States (Jacobson, 2004). In Kentucky, the state-wide partnership, the Prichard Committee, fosters educational reform through the help of students who serve as ambassadors to the public for the reform act (Mitchell, 1996).

Students who are involved in setting educational policy are extremely active people. In Fort Dodge, Iowa, a 16 year old board member takes many of her courses on the internet. Ms. Srinivas is involved in debate, volleyball, tennis, drama, dance, student council, and her county's youth and action committee. She also managed to start a nonprofit charity for elementary schools (Jacobson, 2004). In Kentucky, Eric Mills was the star of the Ambassadors' program. Eric, worked with the administration of his school to develop a council of students to promote the state program. He published a newspaper, *The Road to Success*, that interwove accounts of other outstanding students together with sports stories and group photographs. The typical student newspaper is as likely to talk about the vice-principal as it is to write about an individual student (Mitchell, 1996).

Organizations that are separate from schools develop student leaders who are concerned about creative learning rather than public relations. An art education program for at-risk students, DAREarts, brings student leaders together for creative activities. They are expected to return to the schools from which they are selected and contribute to the school's art program (DAREarts, 2001). Over 300 inner-city and rural students learn through selected days at intervals throughout the school year. The leaders are thought to be able to reach 10,000 students in their schools. DAREarts reaches students in primarily Toronto and Calgary, Canada. The accounts of student leaders are written by the adult leaders of DAREarts. This program tries to link students with their communities. If they are not appreciated, students often want to leave poor communities as soon as they are able to do so.

When students are important to communities, they become active members of community organizations and school councils. Rural communities in Australia are successful in retaining their youth (Kilpatrick, et al., 2002). Schools are an important part of offering specialized certificates for new developments in fishing or farming. In Western Australia at Margaret River High School, regional conferences led to a number of partnership programs that made student leaders central to their concern (Kilpatrick, et al., 2002). This community is a resource for learning, a recycling project, a work experience program, an Enterprise Day that has become a national model for bringing small businesses and students together, community readers for students, and a cadet program for emergency services. Environmental concerns, particularly wild fires, lead to the choice of community service over military training as an aim for student cohorts.

Similar to the Australian experiences, a small group of researchers and activists are training students to survey and express their views in the United States (Olson,

2002). In addition to the usual ways of conducting research, such as questionnaires and interviews, the students utilize videos, contacts through the internet, and differences among schools that are striking to them. Discovering the differences between suburban and inner city schools can motivate different groups of students to work for change (Kennedy Y. E. L. L. Project, 2002).

A small minority of students believe they can influence change in their communities and schools. For the grade eight students, the John W. Gardner Center for Youth and Their Communities at Standford University develops trial efforts (2001). Student leaders find the location of meetings, the problems of traffic in the community, and opportunities to learn more about what adults were planning for students.

Reviewing proposals for the city's housing and human resources committee that awards grants to adults to help students, empowers the students involved. Otherwise, less than 20 percent of students feel they could influence change in their communities or schools (Kennedy Y. E. L. L. Project, 2002). At-risk students learn how to work with adult groups. They learn how to contact family centers to meet their needs. Students also want teachers trained to provide interaction with them, but this is not a high priority for grade eight students.

High school students usually seek recognition, but competition among student groups promotes opportunities to develop their leadership. Where there is competition, they become articulate, learning to speak and write about their education. In Chicago, two rival organizations competed for student support: *New Expression*, an independent newspaper, and Student Alliance, an organization of student representatives who are trying to be a part of school-based management (Mitchell, 1996).

Leaders of both organizations were involved in politics. The editor of the newspaper, Susan Herr, left to join Mayor Daley's staff. The newspaper's volunteer reporters become paid editors and later, as adults, specialists. The founder of the Alliance, Philip Bleicher, was a student representative on the Chicago Board of

Education. Other student activists replaced them. Beginning in 1971, *New Expression* grew to where it published every month over 80,000 copies of its paper. Starting in 1991, a small group of students in the Student Alliance became concerned about educational issues. The Alliance began as a citywide coalition of students in Chicago and, in 1992, started holding national meetings of student representatives on school boards. The Student Alliance is organized around educational rights and educational policy affecting students.

In contrast, *New Expression* is in tune with students' immediate interests, including music and fashion. *New Expression* is accountable to a nonprofit organization, the Youth Commission, which raises foundation funds (New Expressions, 2001-2002). The Youth Commission supports similar papers in New York, Los Angeles, Washington, Atlanta, Boston, and San Francisco. On one important occasion, the Youth Commission supported eight students at *New Expression* in undertaking a report on Chicago schools (Adolf Mendez, interview, May 2, 1995). *Project InSIDER*, by eight students including two dropouts, stressed the need for a greater sense of community between students in many different streams and between staff and students (Mitchell, 1996).

The Youth Commission, with the support of foundations, undertakes other projects to support students. One of its programs, Students United for Participation and Representation, led to the training of fifty students in decision making (Mitchell, 1996). A report on this training and an attempt to implement its recommendations led Philip Bleicher to form the Student Alliance. The Alliance became inactive when Philip Bleicher was unable to account for his expenditures of organizational funds, which became a crisis for him and the organization (Aimee Horton, personal communication, November, 2001).

Without a free press and competition among students, only sporadic attempts to obtain student expression of their ideas are made. The occasional expert on educational reform, such as Ted Sizer, calls for student contributions. Student publications that are supported by regular newspapers, such as the *Calgary Herald*, disappear after a few years (Mitchell, 1996). In Alabama and Australia, students publish rural newspapers when the community has none (Mitchell, 2000; Kilpatrick, et al., 2002). Special circumstances lead to the voices of students being heard.

STUDENT LEADERS

Unlike adults in schools, students leaders are trained for generalized leadership, which frequently means that specific opportunities to empower students are ignored. At no time were students active participants in the research on volunteers, such as that conducted by Big Brothers on their program to mentor deserving students (Mitchell, 1998). Students are not asked whether programs for them should be carried out by individual mentors who decide to help on their own or those who are persuaded to do so by their employers. Involving students in making decisions is seen to be less important than providing the service.

Different groups of students do have ideas about improvements that partnerships might make in their schools. Elementary school students want the appearance of their schools and their playgrounds improved (Meighen, 1986). Working with land architects, at-risk elementary students design their school play areas (Mitchell, 1996). High school students contribute to research by academics (Sarason, 1993), develop new products for industry (Rideout, 1997), and provide accounting services in small towns (Chacon, 1997). However, these examples are exceptional.

In order to create changes in education, several programs create regular links between students and schools. These include peer support systems, leadership development, and peer tutoring. Peer support programs emerge for specific groups, such as the sons and daughters of alcoholics (Mitchell, 2000b). In some communities, support groups operate for both the students and their addicted parents. Student counsellors, rather than professionals, assist students and refer serious problems to experts, but these student volunteers are capable of making unique contributions. More independent activities are developed with students as they become high school seniors.

Compared to peer support, leadership programs are not widely available. These programs focus on student activities, rather than academic achievements. They ignore the specific situations in which leaders evolve and focus on leadership as a part of student development. Important examples of student leaders' work are shown at the annual conference and continuing program of the Canadian Association of Student Activity Advisors. In order to attract student volunteers, organizations needing them hold festivals (Above and Beyond, 2002). This organization's newspaper discussed problems of involving students in band festivals. The most important award for Canadian student volunteers is the Duke of Edinburgh recognition for three different age levels of students.

This Canadian leadership provides curriculum resources for high school students that are similar to those that elementary students receive (Canadian Association of Student Activity Advisors, 2002). Workbooks, handbooks, and suggestions for student activities are published for the advisors of this extracurricular program. The activities cover understanding the stages of group development, directions for using the microphone, and having every student demolish a junk car (Above and Beyond, 2001-2002). Study guides are provided for movies, such as *Lean on Me*, stressing strong leaders. Specific tips for tutoring other students are also added. More individual programs are developed for high school seniors.

Other leadership programs, such as the Best Buddies Leadership Conference, develop techniques to link a variety of students, including those with special needs, with others who are different in other ways. An interesting variation in special education is the peer forum where the more able students are expert members of a panel; the peer forum has been found to be very effective in motivating students for learning (Lewandowski, 1989). Such forums involve academic achievement, self-esteem, and the need for education.

Peer tutoring creates bonds between student tutors and at-risk students in ways that teachers alone could not do. Effective programs exist for disabled students, autistic children, and inner city minority children (Delquadri, 1986). When a special education class is divided into teams, members develop support from the teams and alternate between being the tutor or tutee. Peer tutors are an alternative to direct instruction by teachers to small groups that is expensive.

General peer tutoring is an effective means of empowering both the givers and receivers of tutoring (Mitchell, 1998). At the elementary level, students are given detailed procedures to follow in order to keep the tutor and tutee on task while trying to prevent any put-downs by competitive students. In high schools, the procedures are outlined in greater detail in order to control students. The programs establish positive personal relationships, develop life skills, assist families in overcoming conflicts, and increase interaction with social and cultural groups (National Dropout Prevention Center/Network, n.d.).

A review of over fifty studies shows that peer tutoring by students in elementary and secondary schools is successful in raising examination results (Michael, 1990). The programs increase attendance, decrease drug and alcohol use, improve family relations, decrease early pregnancies, increase entry-level employment, and improve school achievement results. These multiple benefits are a good example of how social indicators can be used for other programs, which is discussed in Chapter 5. However, despite the possible benefits, special awards for students involved in these tasks were not created.

In 1997 at the President's Summit for America's Future, high-level recognition was given to programs for students. A number of adult programs announced they were increasing their support. Big Brothers pledged to double the number of its mentors to 200,000 (Mitchell, 1998). Many volunteers were recruited, including retired teachers, but recognition for students was still lacking. Communities in Schools organized a number of national conferences on health initiatives, including AIDS, but they have also looked elsewhere for volunteers, rather than at student leaders; students were not represented at the conferences.

COMPETITIVE SITUATIONS

Both students and adult volunteer leaders are given greater recognition when there is competition. With competition, the nature of the partnership changes as does the nature of leadership. Under these conditions, cooperation remains possible if it is confined to a select group with common goals, a narrow agenda, and a clear opponent (Rex Hagans, interview, May 13, 1998). There are situations among social service providers, organizations of the disabled, and businesses, where multiple partnerships exist in spite of unstable relationships among the competitors.

The arts frequently compete for limited support, although students want to be involved in them. In Tennessee, three statewide programs combined their resources to form a partnership called *ACT III*. The rivals are the Tennessee Arts Commission, the arts program of the Tennessee Department of Education, and the education program for the Tennessee Performing Arts Center, called the Humanities Outreach in Tennessee (HOT) (Mitchell, 2000a).

The Tennessee Arts Commission provides residencies for artists, recognizes outstanding arts schools, and develops exchanges between teachers and artists. Unlike *New Expressions*, the Tennessee group adopts the perspective of professionals in providing the arts to students. The Tennessee Department of Education carries on an extensive program of in-service education, including its Tennessee Arts Academy, which rewards elementary teachers and high school arts specialists with a free, aesthetic experience in the summer. HOT offers over 40 performances a year to 60,000 students and provides lesson plans to accompany the performances, technical assistance to schools on how to present their own plays, and summer seminars for teachers.

All three partners are involved in professional education for teachers. Their initial project involved writing applications for grants, including both the development of visions and grant writing (Ibid). Subsequent conferences involved incorporating technology into arts education. The directors of the three arts groups share a common philosophy including a belief in an organized curriculum and the necessity for arts specialists in schools (Joe Giles, interview, February 2, 1998; Nancy Shumate, interview, March 16, 1998; Alice Swanson, interview, March 16, 1998).

These three educators are critical of outsiders, particularly the grand approach of the Bernstein Center in Nashville, where all four organizations are located. The Bernstein Center is likely to involve students in more publicized activities. Maintaining their focus, the three partners complement each other and are located near each other. Joe Giles is concerned with people and relationships, Nancy Shumate writes to support the projects, and Alice Swanson looks towards the long-term contribution of current partnerships. Joe Giles works out of a government cubicle; Nancy Shumate has an office in the performing arts center; and Alice Swanson carries out her duties in an art museum.

Each of the partners sees the other as a necessary component in *ACT III*. Nancy Schumate says Joe Giles knows the teachers; Alice Swanson knows the artists and through her organization, the Tennessee Performing Arts Center, she provides resources (Interview, March 16, 1998). Each secures a contribution from their separate organization to a common budget. Their meetings are geared to specific tasks to which students are to respond.

ALLIANCES

While arts organizations hedge their competition with limited partnerships, business alliances avoid competition. Many businesses develop programs with educators that provide resources and financial help, but focus on older students who may become employees or consumers (Mitchell, 1996). For their directed and limited aims, business organizations coordinate their efforts to avoid duplication (National Alliance of Business, 1991). As discussed in Chapter 2, the Business Roundtable (BRT) is the most important business organization affecting educational reform. It is part of an intricate web of business groups, which are as distant from students as history dates .

The BRT collaborates with the National Alliance of Business and other organizations (Mitchell, 1996). The Business Alliance considers any company that pays its dues as a member, in contrast to the BRT, which has only eighty-nine select members. The Alliance prepares publications and offers conferences that the BRT supports. Both of these American organizations are members of the Business

Coalition on Education Reform, as are the Committee on Economic Development and the Chamber of Commerce. The Committee on Economic Development includes 250 CEOs and senior managers, grant makers, and community leaders. The Chamber of Commerce has a large membership and many local and regional affiliates. Although the Center for Workforce Preparation is part of the Chamber of Commerce, it raises its own funds and provides studies and conferences to individual chambers relating to school financing and technology.

The business organizations deviate from activities that support their own interests when they rely on outside experts or see their narrow interests depend on community survival, such as during race riots. The institutional survival of business is more important than the profit margins of individual companies. The position of the BRT and the Alliance is developed by an educator, David Hornbeck, who has served as a chief administrator in Philadelphia and Maryland and advised Kentucky on its extensive program of educational reform (Mitchell, 1998). Early childhood education is an aim of the BRT since it returns its investment several times over, but early education is evaluated in business terms.

In Chicago, where racial tensions and other community issues cannot be avoided, the most important business group, the Civic Committee, undercut its own advocacy organization, Leadership for Quality Education (Mitchell, 1996). The Civic Committee joined with conservative political interests and abandoned the cause of promoting democratic participation that other advocacy groups were seeking. Lawrence Howe, the established lawyer for Bell and Howell, decided this committee's fate as Executive Director of the Civic Committee.

In Canada, education is not a priority for national business interests. The Business Council on National Issues (BCNI) is similar to the Business Roundtable in that it is composed of the executives of the largest corporations (Ted Mieszkalski, interview, August 24, 1994). The BCNI was a crucial supporter of free trade debate and influenced the number of televised debates on the subject. In education, the BCNI commissioned a few studies, such as one on job retraining, and a position paper on competitiveness. The chief executive of BCNI, Tom D'Acquino, does not use his position as a platform to influence educational reform. BRT, the American counterpart, on the other hand, has a ten-year commitment to keep educational reform as its highest priority and various executives support its aims.

Leaders who share a common vision among large organizations will work with outsiders to develop a coherent policy. Both Tom D'Acquino in Canada and Lawrence Howe in Chicago differ from the leaders of BRT who gave David Hornbeck the leeway to develop an educational philosophy for them. The ten-year commitment of the BRT to educational reform is similar to a guarantee. Neither the Canadian nor American business alliances appreciate the social significance of education for students.

The three arts organizations in Tennessee are closer to students because of their common philosophy that calls for participation in the arts (Mitchell, 2000). They had the same expert mentor, Jeff Patchen, the executive director of the regional Getty program for many years. Mr. Patchen overrode the old structural approach of disciplined or structured arts education to include progressive approaches. He developed an alliance with Columbia College in South Carolina for a regional dance program that no arts group has in the Southern states. His philosophy led the prospective partners to see the advantages of cooperation.

In addition to a shared vision, broader cooperation requires organizations to expand the group that is involved. The creation of a coordinating agency, which is separate from the original partners, is a positive step (Mitchell, 1996). Kentucky, with its broad-based educational reform, created the Partnership for Kentucky School Reform that operates with the Prichard Committee. This partnership is a model for the Business Roundtable, which sent a new education director there for training. This organization includes business, civic, government, education, and union leaders. This collaboration extends to the Council on Science and Technology. Partnerships with parents have been actively developed with the aid of foundation grants. These reforms aim to involve citizens under the aegis of community and business leaders.

Kentucky bases its research center at the University of Kentucky. University leaders play a key role in the expansion of many different partnerships. Universities are as important today as were the churches in the past in persuading the unconvinced to accept new partnerships. Chicago has organized a council of universities who are committed to their reform effort (Mitchell, 1996). Educational change involves more than individual faculty members.

VISIONARY LEADERS

Partnerships require mobilizing support that is beyond the scope of universities. Implementation of collaboration depends on the collective ability to manage change among different kinds of organizations. In order to sustain collaboration, a way to assure funding, environmental scanning and adaptation, and communication within the partnerships must be found (Mitchell, 2001a). Boundary spanning occurs at the edges of organizations to solve joint problems. Adult leaders are more able to guide youth because they are aware of additional opportunities in the environment. Leaders perceive new issues; they see and suggest solutions across organizational boundaries; and they arise on the basis of competence and credibility rather than formal positions.

Principals who occupy this role are distracted by other matters over time (Kilpatrick, et al., 2002). However, acceptance of a partnership is tenuous if another staff member coordinates partnerships. Collaboration is more enhanced if the coordinator is now an administrator who in the past has played multiple community roles. It is also important for partnership to become a part of the curriculum that requires the involvement of a variety of staff members. Leaders for partnerships are a new breed who function broadly and as a part of other groups.

Partnerships require boundary spanners who communicate within and across organizations. Often they have experience with different kinds of organizations. These new leaders engage in a variety of activities that support the new organization, protect their own organizations, or link organizations together. Working as fellows, boundary spanners see the situation, act rapidly, and use their imagination to develop alternatives (Sarason & Lorentz ,1998). Such coordinators see the limits of their own organization's culture and are able to go beyond it. They "bend the rules" in order to alter the agenda of the school (Schorr, 1997). These leaders challenge authorities, look for similar fellows within their own or other organizations, and seek permission to travel.

Boundary spanners create reactions against themselves (Mitchell, 2002). Their personal contacts are their base for cooperation. Visions or policy positions provide support in the activists within their own and partner organizations. The coordinators of change are successful when they build strong communication networks to anticipate and solve potential conflicts. They are especially important in Aboriginal education or cross-cultural situations (Cathy Littlejohn-King, personal communication, August 22, 2002). Boundary spanners create synchronized administrative procedures with common goals.

The difference between two North Carolina districts shows the importance of goals in order to integrate social services with schools (Mitchell, 2001a). In only one district does boundary spanning consist of regular searches for new approaches, continuous communication, and changing policies. Both districts experienced changes in superintendents and other leadership positions, which shows the importance of consistent approaches.

In one district with a shared vision, one key boundary spanner is an early childhood educator. As a teacher, principal, and Director of Federal Programs, this activist participated in the initial needs assessment efforts. In her original position as an early childhood educator, she built support for pre-kindergarten education, planned parent education, and programs to promote parent involvement. In her later role as Director of Federal Programs, she accesses many funding sources to put different "pieces" in place, including a Title One preschool program, Reading Recovery programs, and an Even Start initiative (L. Bradshaw, personal communication, December 14, 2000). These systemic results demonstrate how the Director of Federal Programs links available opportunities to new efforts. Her ability to share information and maintain support within the school district assures success for a number of programs. This leader is a visionary and the program of integrated services continues to evolve as a result of her contributions together with the district's policy.

THE COMMUNITY SPIRIT

The problems and possibilities of community leaders are revealed by their role in integrated services. The best example of such leadership is that of the former American President, Jimmy Carter, in the *Atlanta Project* (Mitchell, 1996; Mitchell, 1998). This project organizes clusters of community resources around individual schools so that the entire city is covered by them. For example, the *Atlanta Project* mobilized 12,000 volunteers to identify 17,000 children who need immunization shots. The Atlanta Project also brings volunteers together around crises in health and education, such as pimps luring girls as young as ten into prostitution.

The Carter Center uses drama in order to mobilize support for its initiative among students and their parents (Mitchell, 2000a). Partners for one of its projects, which involves guns and violence, include the Alliance Theater, the Atlanta School System and the Turner Broadcasting System. Many other businesses provide support, such as BellSouth, which leads a major literacy effort. The Carter Center is mobilizing volunteers as part of a national effort to transform the *Atlanta Project* into *Project America.*

In Chicago, a similar attempt at integrating parks, schools, housing projects, and police into community clusters failed (Greg Darnieder, interview, October 17, 1993). A friendship group of executives from the four institutions was promising, but when the top executives changed, interest in the Chicago cluster project disappeared (Mitchell, 1996). The problem in the Chicago case was that middle-level managers did not create their own cluster because they are prone to isolation and competition. Similar problems occur among specialists working with large school boards or departments of education (Mitchell, 1998). Those caught up in administration, their specialities, or their careers need the dedication of volunteers. In a striking case, executives from a high-technology company failed to develop any support within their organization for a partnership that they desired with a university (Ginsburg, et al, 2004).

For their part, volunteers and students need to learn to be more like executives in decision making if they are to change either the non-profit organizations where they provide services or the governmental agencies that are among their partners. Public policy change is described as reinventing government, finding alternatives to bureaucracy and rules in education (Osborne & Gaebler, 1992). The pioneers among volunteers and non-governmental agencies supporting the discovery of alternatives are experimenting at becoming active decision makers (Brown, 1995).

Although they may not be making schools into open, competitive, and risk-taking organizations, volunteers are themselves entering into new, uncertain, and changing positions. The first generation of volunteers are inventors, if not entrepreneurs. Volunteers connect students to the adult world (Mitchell, 1998). Volunteers bond with the students; for example, seniors talk about students with whom they work as their children or buddies.

A caring norm is developed for students, a model for the future. Although it may take a generation for the volunteer's gifts to be repaid, their commitment changes the climate of schools. For example, tolerance for individual and cultural differences increases as a result of cooking demonstrations by ethnic minorities when the cooking lessons are part of a process of learning about other families (Brown, 1995; Mitchell, 1995). In Louis Armstrong Elementary School in New York City, male readers are recruited to read to students who lack male parents (Mitchell, 1998). On Vancouver Island, volunteer coordinators provide a wide variety of skill and art classes at noon (Brown, 1995). Volunteers often remain involved with students long after their children leave the schools.

In many places, the commitment of volunteers is in itself an inspiration to children and staff in schools. In Edmonton, Canada, a social studies and mathematics teacher, Bill McKenzie, was diagnosed with terminal cancer. Instead of giving up, he became a volunteer for the public board, teaching the arts; three years later, he is alive and active (Interview, May 8, 1997). In California, a mother, Kika Wilson, created an art education program for the local elementary school. With school permission, Mrs. Wilson organizes two dozen parents, gathers materials, provides workshops on creating lesson plans, and teaches art in each class weekly (Bradley, Sack, Manzo & Ponessa, 1997).

Volunteers are encouraged by members of community organizations, but experts often believe that such people are already too busy. In Chicago, Mary Lou Schmidt, a medical doctor, is able to coordinate the art education partnerships at Hawthorne Elementary School because she is a master in delegating specific tasks to other people (Interview, June 7, 1996). Dr. Schmidt is busy with her practice, her research, and her family. However, if you want to get a job done, find a busy person who knows how to deal with a situation in which she is overworked (Mitchell, 1990).

Volunteers are empowered by their involvement and are able to do more than they previously imagined; educators are strengthened as well. The decision to involve volunteers in the schools is made by principals in order to get "people on your side" (Brown, 1995, p. 38). The principals encourage volunteers in small ways, such as giving up their parking space for these contributors or meeting them in the halls before they reach their office. Participation by volunteers is also promoted by creating a parents' room and a volunteer coordinator. However, volunteers create their own system to link themselves together, such as immigrants sponsoring newcomers from the same ethnic group (Brown, 1995).

Most principals who initiate the volunteer programs believe that they are community orientated (Brown, 1995). In contrast to bureaucratic patterns, those in the volunteers' schools promote the causes in which they believe and recognize people as being different. Businesspeople, who complain about school executives being rule-bound and cautious, should recognize this set of principals as risk-takers (Mitchell, 1996). Innovative business executives are often sought as partners by risk-taking principals (Michael, 1990).

Aside from seeking business partners, active principals bring in a volunteer coordinators who changes the program as well as create contacts with many individual and group partners. Similar coordinators are involved with family centers, which are the focus of service integration. Both organizers find ways to deal with perceived needs (Mitchell, 1996). Volunteer coordinators relate to many issues as they happen, while the organizers of integrated services confront crises. Coordinators for family centers are responsible for a number of formal activities, such as family education; however, when they directly intervene with client problems, such as the electricity being cut off in winter, they are most inventive.

Kentucky has one of the best developed programs of family resource centres, but few volunteers are involved to augment the work of professionals (Susan Schweder, interview, May 8, 1995). The desire to deal with immediate issues is the overriding goal of those who develop the program (Judy Carter, interview, May 1, 1995). Coordinators deal with pressing client concerns, but do not invest in developing volunteers. Two students who are on the board of such centers are able to talk to each other, but are not encouraged to form a common front with parents and community members. Volunteers are able to reach children and families concerning a variety of problems that people do not want to reveal to experts (Mitchell, 2000b). It is in an exceptional group of mixed professionals that maintains an exchange of social greetings, such as hi-fives (Jacobsen & Gladstone, 2004)

Some volunteers are able to contribute to decision making for partnerships. Unlike Kentucky, in Boston, an independent board selects volunteers who effectively integrate social services and the school (Michael, 1990). In San Francisco, volunteers designed a racial integration plan acceptable to the constituent groups, after the professionals failed (Mitchell, 1990). Volunteers are involved in school councils, which in places such as Chicago, decide school policies and select principals. In poor countries, such as Pakistan, volunteers raise funds and organize village committees so there can be schools available (Rizvi and Sayee, 2004).

In all countries, professionals resist the volunteers' influence and attempts to set policy. The Kentucky program of integrated services does not draw on volunteers because the criteria for awarding grants to support the centers omits them from a checklist (Mitchell, 1996). Ironically, parents and students constitute the majority of the boards for such Kentucky centers. The non-profit organization that influenced the development of the Kentucky program, Cities in Schools, originated as a program for volunteers and regularly emphasizes the contribution of these volunteers.

NON-PROFIT ORGANIZATIONS

Cities in Schools, formerly called Communities in Schools (CIS), is a high profile independent organization that influences educational reform, involving efforts to link schools with social agencies (Mitchell, 1998). CIS is a major influence on the development of the Atlanta Project and family resource centers in Kentucky (Marsha Morganti, interview, May, 5, 1995). It received support from President Bush as well as former presidents Carter, Bush, and Clinton (Mitchell, 2000a). CIS is involved in the Chicago reform movement and its efforts for social services provided by schools (Janet Hudolin, interview, May 15, 1995).

CIS creates local programs through the use of volunteers, but carries out centralized publicity efforts under the leadership of its founder, Bill Millikin. Aside from political leaders, CIS draws contributions and endorsements from entertainers and sports personalities. Each year, leading musical artists record a song or music on video, or add 25 cents to the price of concert tickets to support CIS (Mitchell, 1998). The entertainment industry helps CIS through scholarship programs, national music competitions, and special concerts. The support of athletes is spectacular; after each Super Bowl, the National Football League creates a CIS academy. This high-level approach could reward local efforts.

Since 1977, CIS has created programs for young people in trouble, most recently those suffering from AIDS (Mitchell, 1998). The founder, long-time director and current chairman of the board, Bill Milliken, comes from the streets of Pittsburgh, beginning with a street ministry in Harlem. (Business Week, 1989). This former dropout started street academies for students who drop out of schools. Initially, he used tutoring programs and alternative schools and later developed social and health services within regular schools. Academy sponsors include the U. S. Postal Service and Department of Justice, Burger King, Goldman Sachs, and National Football League. Corporate support comes from General Foods, BellSouth, GTE, Amoco, Coca-Cola, and Federated Department Stores.

With high profile support, CIS builds independent programs (Lewis, 1991). Milliken wants to avoid "paternalistic helping" and "parachuting in the experts" from government or other centralized agencies. As a part of community initiatives, volunteers are mentors, tutors and facilitators within schools. In Chicago, a board is led by a local businessperson and consists of educators, religious leaders, health and social service representatives, and other businesspeople. Bill Milliken sees these organizations as mediating structures, replacing the ties lost by the decline of religious institutions and the extended family.

In less developed countries with extended families, such as Pakistan, a few powerful groups are able to dominate educational change (Mitchell, Klinck, &Burger, 2004). The Aga Khan Foundation and its network of organizations links with elite universities, such as Oxford. In more developed countries, like Mexico, non-governmental organizations may become independent, which can be such an important step that it leads to change in governments. Linking organizations is a problem for advanced societies in the North to worry about; in the South the dominant groups are often tightly linked (Rizvi & Sayee, 2004).

ESTABLISHED ORGANIZATIONS

In North America, there are many lower-profile organizations mobilizing volunteers for school related partnerships. Many of the these organizations have consistent external evaluations, such as Big Brothers (Opinion Research Centre, 1995). Others, such as the National Parent Teachers' Association (PTA), are so well accepted that education would be unimaginable without them (Mitchell, 1998).

The organizations, supported by research evidence, focus on a specific program, such as tutoring students. The established programs are based on general assumptions about schooling, such as the importance of creative work for students.

Established programs depend on the interests of volunteers; specialized ones may be encouraged by employers or rewarded by the community.

Although neither type of program directly appeals to students, controversies and major social changes attract their interests. The traditional suppliers of volunteers, the National Parent Teachers' Association and the Junior League, are showing signs of new initiatives (Mitchell, 1998). The PTA is a member of an association, which fights for educational reforms and opposes budget cuts in education. It opposes the commercialization of education. School-based management leads parents to concentrate on local fundraising and local organizations (Mitchell, 2000a). Such parents question their support for a state or national organization. They do not wish to provide remote groups with dues.

The Junior League brings volunteers into schools to promote social, artistic and attitudinal changes(Mitchell, 1998). In order to continue its efforts, the League must involve professionals and business. In a number of its programs, including arts education, the League has been replaced by professionals. Indeed, this organization has always tried to find specialists to replace them, but this has not always been possible. In 1973, the Junior League in Calgary started Music Alive, a program, which brought musicians to students to teach music appreciation (Goods, 1996). In the 1980s, this program was turned over to a local radio station that terminated it after a change in managers.

Volunteering is becoming a specialized function and advocacy groups are promoting the volunteer or independent sector (O'Connell, 1997). In 1956, the first efforts towards an organization to seek volunteers for schools began with the creation of a citizens' advocacy group in New York City, the Public Education Association (PEA) (Michael, 1990). The PEA started a service to train tutors to help students learn to read. In 1959 and 1964, the Ford Foundation gave PEA a grant, first to expand the program in the city and, later, to create a national effort.

In 1975, the National School Volunteer Program received a sustaining grant from the Edna McConnell Clark Foundation. In 1988, the National School Volunteer

Program merged with a similar organization to form the National Association of Partners in Education. This latter organization continued to provide training materials, conferences, and research on partnerships (2001).

Parents want an active role in education, refusing to remain a part of the supporting cast. In the 1980s, racial and educational crises in education brought out volunteers who would be critical of the system (Mitchell, 1996). In the 1990s, the so called "Ninja parents" started demanding and getting a say about the operation of schools; they hired additional teachers themselves (Mitchell, 1998).

Single issues or events are catalysts that ignite the reaction of many parents. Religion and sex touch a nerve among some parents. Parents in Sacramento believe classical myths are witchcraft that should not be taught (Ibid). Community members in Michigan became agitated about the removal of references to God and morality in a mission statement as are politicians about the removal of God in "In God We Trust." Parents may also react to curriculum or organizational changes. Parents in St. Louis oppose the 'new, new mathematics' recommended in the report of the National Council of Teachers of Mathematics. Parents react against things that schools do or issues that parents themselves raise, but do not know what their own aims are for education, or even if they want to be involved in the operation of schools. In Alberta, Canada, parents do not want to serve on councils or have the councils hire the principal (Mitchell, 1996).

Rather than reacting against an issue, parents may contribute to education on a continuing basis. If they do so, they begin to think about education as a growth experience for their children as well as providing opportunities within their communities. Parents move from concern for their own children to consideration of how other students may be helped. Once involved in the broader web, parents develop specific skills for themselves and their children. They enforce policies on their children, such as limits on television viewing. They accept school policies until events lead them to question them. Parents realize educational improvement, test courses, and evaluation of schools are involved in the opportunities that schools provide for their children's future as well as for others.

Active volunteers in schools make the transition to broader concerns about children and learning (Brown, 1995). Parents are often satisfied with schools and do not realize how much they are misled by teacher grading as compared to standardized examination results (Office of Educational Research and Improvement, U.S. Department of Education, 1992). Activists see how much more schools may do, and know enough about the schools to make changes possible. Parents who are involved as volunteers over a long period of time have influence at the school, including grading policies (Mitchell, 1998). All parents are in a position to support educational policies or undermine efforts by withdrawing their children or withholding their support.

As a result of particular events, such as teacher strikes or budget cuts, parents are taking responsibility on themselves for education. In some communities, parents are formally evaluating teachers (Mitchell, 1998). In other communities, parents organize their own internet sites as a basis for circulating information about their schools. Parents are no longer dependent on administrators for information about school operations, teacher behavior, and student performance.

Students are similarly becoming militant. In Boston, they have demonstrated against the state's examination policy (Mitchell, 2000a). In Chicago, students have deliberately failed exams, obtained a grant from a foundation, and organized a conference with the help of experts to attack the preoccupation with testing. The access of schools to parents and students means that the profession is influenced by their clients.

A variety of other groups are joining the consumer movement in education while they are volunteering to help with schools. Retirees are expected to assist schools as a replacement for mothers who are working outside the home. They are a potential for education that is barely tapped. Current volunteers devote less than an hour per week to volunteering (Freedman, 1994). In Australia, retirees in rural communities have become readers in schools (Kilpatrick, et al., 2002). Retirees provide the perspective of their experience, but their involvement may lead to criticism of school policies because they identify more with students than with the school and want schools to achieve their goals rather than follow their ritualistic procedures.

An exemplary program in Salt Lake City, Utah, Senior Motivators in Learning and Education Services (SMILES), focuses on monitoring students' attendance and work habits (Mitchell, 1998). Other programs involve retirees actively. A program that would make seniors active and critical, Linking Lifetimes, matches blue-collar elders who experienced problems with youths who are in trouble with the justice system. These elders are "like walking-life-skills curricula" (Friedman, 1994, p. 32). While increasing the attendance and achievements of youth, seniors improve their own abilities to think and communicate (Strom & Strom, 1995). There is now a curriculum guide for grandparents who may be raising their grandchildren.

ADVOCACY

As is true for programs involving seniors, volunteer efforts could break the mould of existing programs in schools. In a program for scientists and engineers in Washington, D.C., teachers were encouraged to write job descriptions for specialized volunteers, find an effective match between themselves and the volunteer experts and form an overview committee of community representatives (Michael, 1990). These are minimum steps for a variety of volunteer programs.

In order to make major changes in education, volunteer organizations need to establish links to larger or more powerful organizations. Local advocacy groups are the heart of volunteer efforts in education. As discussed in Chapter 5, students may study the most successful advocates and help communities develop policies for the future. Organization of the World Alliance for Citizen Participation is light years away from parents and community members in most local communities (O'Connell, 1997).

Community organizers can articulate the problems of local communities. Parents may aid schools, such as in a program in a poor Baltimore community where volunteers train students in different styles of art (Mitchell, 1998). In Nashville, which calls itself *Music City*, there were no music teachers until 1995. Parents organized in teams to teach music or hired a teacher themselves (Mitchell, 2000a). In cities such as Seattle and Chicago, where educators trained radical groups, such as the Industrial Areas Foundation (IAF), a whole series of changes are being made in education.

Designs for Change is a research organization that transformed itself into an action group by employing organizers trained by radicals (Mitchell, 1996). Designs for Change is interested in the problems of special education students. Local parent and community groups are trained, by Designs for Change, to argue issues and initiate court cases. In this situation, parent and community groups are the shock troops for the advocacy organization. The director of Designs for Change, Don Moore, does not believe that student activists are important enough for their phone calls to be returned. Advocacy groups obtain support and recognition from foundations and governments for community volunteers.

Some reform organizations remain hesitant to accept volunteers. In the arts, where professional status is marginal, this quandary is striking. For example, David O'Fallon, director of the Minnesota Center for Arts Education, could only mention folk arts as a legitimate arena for those who did not have a professional background (Interview, June 12, 1996). The volunteer who is accepted is an exception. Bill McKenzie, the teacher diagnosed with terminal cancer, was the only volunteer given a responsible position with the Edmonton public system (Sharon Busy, interview, May 8, 1977). A number of volunteers may be prominent in the start of a reform effort, but no new ones are later added to the inner core (Mitchell, 2000a). Professional educators in the arts rejected opportunities I provided them to state their suggestions for change, since they might be perceived as radical (Mitchell, 2000a). Volunteers in the arts do reveal a religious-like calling that could be mobilized into programs for change.

MERGING PARTNERS

The challenge is to link volunteers with protégés or other people within organizations. Unlike professionals, volunteers cannot be controlled by organizations, and are feared by some administrators for this reason. Volunteers are an effective link between students and educators as well as other professionals. Volunteers can join with professionals to reach high-risk clients since some clients will know them and confide in them (Mitchell, 1996, Mitchell 2000b). Social agencies, businesses, and the higher professions may create effective councils of partners when the councils include elected officers or volunteers from the community.

In spite of the potential for involving volunteers and developing a greater sense of community, those presently planning integrated services think like businesspeople rather than family members (Mitchell, 1996). In Kentucky, the form required by the state for government grants to family resource centers does not require service by volunteers; in spite of a philosophy of community support, this omission means there are few volunteers. In Alberta, Canada, the emphasis on reinventing government as a basis for integrated services involves saving money rather than serving people. In Chicago, only exceptional individuals transcend the boundaries that professionals maintain. Lawyers refuse to let a paralegal assist parent councils.

Volunteers might link with professional aids and both could establish ties with professionals for community service. In the U.S., early childhood education led to over a million mothers being trained as teachers (Mitchell, 1990). Other links emerge when schools are open to volunteers. Family resource centers welcome at-risk parents who were not previously accepted inside schools (Mitchell, 1998). Parents are members of partner organizations with schools, but the families and informal groups of volunteers are not always accepted themselves.

Parents' involvement and that of other partners evolves from obtaining information on raising their own children to participation in school decisions (Mitchell, 1998). Parents can be further reached by collaborating with community groups who provide services to them and to their children, which may not be available from schools. Parents may be more than committee members, while other partners from the community may move in to be committee members. Businesses show their initial interests by adopting a school or providing for retail shops in schools (Mitchell, 1996). The arts try and win acceptance by concentrating on enhancing the basic skills of students through the integration of creative approaches in the teaching of every subject (Mitchell, 2000a).

Communication between the school and partners depends on the ways the facilitators respond to them. The principal, who encourages volunteers, is modeling the ways to empower people. Business and social agencies may show concern for students by providing free breakfasts for at-risk students. External partners learn from the school staff. If the coordinator is providing emergency services, this is a change in the image and character of schools. Continuous communication means that the coordinator is linking the school with its supporters and there is a sharing of points of view.

Communication with different partners allows parents to share their perspectives on students with retirees, businesspeople, or diverse professionals. In order to change schools, parents need broader issues that appeal to the other constituents (Mitchell, 1990). Parents must merge their view of children in families with the business executives' perspective of students as future employees (Mitchell, 1996). Future employees are visible by the end of high school, but the problems of difficult students begin before the end of the elementary grades, which is why businesses need to view the entire school experience as others do.

By middle school, job shadowing and cooperative work-study programs make the world of work meaningful to students. The Information Technology Association of Canada believes there is a natural progression from school sponsorship in elementary grades to career programs in secondary schools and, in turn, to cooperative research at the post-secondary level (Mitchell, 1996). At every stage, the individual interest of students is reconcilable with the perspectives of business and technology.

When developed freely, volunteering provides a basis for such reconciliation. Volunteers participate to help others, act on the basis of a cause, seek something that is personally satisfying, or look for a sense of accomplishment (Duchesne, 1989). The idealism of volunteers is an antidote to practical or personal interests of business leaders or parents.

For parents, a focus upon learning activities at home requires other steps before it promotes active decision making in schools (Mitchell, 1998). Families reading together is a limited achievement, compared to having parents, teachers, and children each writing as a part of the National Writing Program (Mitchell, 1998). Businesspeople have come into schools to teach practical writing and to show their own personal interests in literature. At-risk students who brag about not writing in schools are surrounded by volunteers who set an opposite example for them.

Volunteers are creating a model for students to help them transcend their own self interest. When volunteers continue to help after their own children have graduated, they are accepted and consulted about the school's plans. As shown in Chapter 2, volunteers may overcome the differences between the social class background of school professionals and people in the communities they serve. As partners become more involved with schools, stereotypes are shattered.

Training teachers to work with parents prevents discrimination against poorer families or single-parent mothers (Mitchell, 1990). Training of parents and volunteers together in the arts overcomes the barrier that separates teachers from other community members (Mitchell, 2000a). This is similar to joint training of teachers and their principals, particularly where the teachers critique the teaching of the principal in order to develop a common language (Mitchell, 1990). Businesspeople, similarly, see principals as less rule bound than themselves; executives come to see school administration as caught in the web of school politics. Businesspeople in high technology are appreciated as education idealists because both groups see themselves as a part of a dramatic change in schools and society (Jacobsen & Gladstone, 2002).

The involvement of partners requires inclusion in decision making. Like the Tennessee arts consortium, partnerships create a common language, joint training, and common budgets (Melville & Blank, 1993). When a few steps are taken, the returns are substantial. When lawyers, accountants, and educators are involved in training parent leaders for school councils, they emerge as active decision makers in education (Mitchell, 1996). In Chicago, when the Algebra Project demonstrates algebra as an alternative over general mathematics for students' futures in ways parents on councils understand, an enormous number of individual parents, as well as those on school councils, wanted their schools to participate in the algebra program (O'Neill & Valenzuela, 1992). Innovations that people want and understand will be accepted.

Participation in community services enhances other partnerships. Integrated services may involve services for clients, programs, or policy integrations. Policy integrations reflect a philosophy of government and organizational change (Mitchell, 1996). Most of the efforts at integration focus on paper programs. Group casework and a common location of services for people are among the few efforts directed at clients. Case work is the core of the Community in Schools (CIS) approach (Mitchell, 1998). For CIS or other organizations, parental decision making about any of the different kinds of integration to be undertaken is minimal.

In places demonstrating dramatic changes in education, parents and volunteers are included in school governance. Kentucky requires an advisory board with two students, parents, and community members for each of the family centres. Chicago has active parent coordinators who are representatives of the community. Parent coordinators are responsible for meeting the needs of high-risk students. Volunteers have a voice when the coordinator acts as their spokesperson and links with advocacy organizations or broader alliances. Otherwise, professionals make decisions and lay persons resist or 'vote with their feet.'

Parents and volunteers want experts to supplement their own views. Parents welcome the opportunity to discuss the discipline of children with one another, but not in parenting programs designed by experts (Mitchell, 1996). Community members believe education should be geared to the basics required for ordinary jobs that they know about, not the experts' view that education for future growth requires science and mathematics for their children (Immerwahr, Johnson & Kernan-Schloss, 1991). Discipline in their homes and careers they know for their children are the concerns of parents surveyed. Students seek to understand their present identity as much as future positions.

When immediate learning is related to future success, the views of educational experts and parents will coincide, as in the Algebra Project. Business leaders and other partners with high status assume they know best, thinking scientists from industry could teach science in schools. When business leaders are themselves in trouble, those who turn the company around talk to those who do the work, including the janitor (Graham, 1992). Executives and professionals similarly need to acquire the view of those who make schools work. Students and their parents give meaning to education as recipients. Educators, as well the external leaders, need to understand that, for parents, the moral development of their children is their primary goal (Immerwahr, Johnson & Kernan-Schloss, 1991). Students want peer support as well as parent support and supervision, particularly at the junior high level (Kennedy Y. E. L. L. Project, 2002).

Mutual learning and respect are important goals for partnership programs. For example, when teachers are given responsibility for reducing environmental waste, they empower students to obtain community support; both teachers and students are strengthened when the government applauds their efforts (Kilpatrick, et al., 2002). The difference between a businesslike or instrumental approach and a community or individual effort involves an understanding of how money, people, and ideas are coordinated. A combination of the expanding relationships and knowledge of change is sometimes referred to as "social capital" (Brown, 1995). The acquisition of such capital by students is critical.

CULTURAL DIFFERENCES

In broader settings, Europeans see the possibilities of partnerships in both the immediate scene and society at large (Nelson & Zadek, 2000). National meetings are held to develop consensus. Local efforts require a broader framework in order to be significant. In the past, Europeans stressed national programs for education with large-scale organizations, such as parents in national assemblies, to influence educational policy (Beattie, 1985). Now they develop local partnerships. On an island in Estonia, a former part of the centralized approach of the Soviet Union, government, business, and a new non-governmental organization are cooperating in order to create jobs for special education youths (Mortensen, 2001).

Collaboration at both the national and local levels is a European-wide effort conducted by the Copenhagen Centre and supported by the Danish government, to promote partnerships across the continent. Europeans are also linking with Americans in partnerships in limited areas, such as the sciences and arts. For example, the Scottish Arts Council is working with Chicago partnerships. An exceptional district in British Columbia, Canada, is advised by Australians and assists the Chinese (Mitchell, 2002). Global patterns will emerge from these exceptions.

The Europeans lead these developments because of their greater experience with partnerships and their ability to overcome extreme positions among partners. Europeans, similar to those in many other countries, see partnerships as a way of achieving greater inclusion with respect to a variety of marginal groups. Because of the history of joint planning between labour and management, their partnerships try to bring antagonists together (Nelson & Zadek, 2000). For example, environmentalists and businesses form a common front up to the point that corporations lose money or environmentalists stop being independent critics. Opponents become allies when limited objectives are pursued to improve the public perceptions of both parties. The cultural differences in the views of partnerships between Europeans and North Americans is a basis for a critical examination of partnerships.

The expansion of partnerships provides an opportunity to consider whether they are contributing to education. Changes might also be considered, such as the addition of arts groups under a policy of inclusion, which seems to apply only to the disabled or immigrants. Drawing on American experience, groups that are not recognized by capitalism, such as volunteers, may be a focus for partnerships. On the other hand, Americans and Canadians are upset when village groups, as in Pakistan, do not increase the education achievement of girls, believing perhaps that the schools, often without regular teachers, are not safe (Rizvi & Sayee, 2004). Reconstructing society through schools is difficult.

REFLECTIONS

Leadership is a slippery subject that requires fitting pieces together. Leadership roles should empower followers or constituents (Gardner, 1990). As have-not students or parents become leaders, the previous generation of leaders learns how effective they can be. This is why Bill Milliken of CIS is so concerned about evidence for his organization's results.

Managers are necessary to run schools or other organizations but they cannot claim to be leaders. Leaders change others in their society and future generations; this is the measure of effective leadership (Gardner, 1990). Thus, partnerships are an important test of leadership. To have an influence requires a vision for the partnerships that constituents work to achieve. The Tennessee arts group, *ACT III*, links arts, education, and their city into a separate entity for its limited goals.

ACT III is an example of organization theory where integration, rather than the pooling of functions, occurs (Thompson, 1967). Integrated organizations involve a mutual adjustment of expectations and roles. Business alliances where partners supplement each other are an example of pooling. Neither a common budget nor common training are required for cooperation, as opposed to collaboration; a pooling of individual resources is the aim. The third form of organizational coordination, a sequence, is most important in creating cooperation among partners for the development of children. Sequences of coordination are critical for multiple partnerships, unlike the industrial use of the model for an assembly line linking different sets of workers.

Models from organizational theory do not account for the variety of leadership differences in an age of partnerships. Attempts to replicate the Carter project show how important one charismatic leader is, how difficult it is to sustain a group of leaders, and how inconsistent the perspectives of middle-level managers are. The dedication of volunteers makes leadership possible, which is not the case with specialists.

Our society emphasizes expertise at the expense of sensitivity to people. Voluntary organizations tend to become selective and task centred. Thus, parents are more instrumental in their decision making. They become concerned for results for their own children and about the issues involved as they make the transition to school issues from concern about individual children. Seniors may provide a concern for others as they realize themselves. Personal concern and involvement is restored by active seniors who relate their difficult times with those of at-risk students. Sympathy and understanding are necessary to overcome misfortune.

Volunteers maintain the human concern, and link personal dedication through political leadership. The task of leaders is to articulate this link, the core of a visionary belief. Moral concern is the base of parents and volunteers that help them to overcome the limitations of experts. Non-profit organizations of volunteers lead to broader contact between people in different societies.

The difference among cultures can lead to many challenges and mandates for leaders involved with partnerships. In Europe, partnerships are sustained in some cases for more than a hundred years, showing how minute are those in the U.S. that exist for three years. On the continent, partnerships include marginal groups that are a serious problem in North America. Countries in the South try and reach marginal religious and ethnic groups (Mitchell, et al., 2004). Vision concerning social change is a reason to relate local voluntary efforts to national efforts.

Mobilizing people behind national efforts requires the convergence of a number of movements from the grass roots, which is the task of leaders who develop organizations. Knowledge of the potential for organizations, such as CIS, and individuals, including Dr. Mary Schmidt, who organized the art program, is an awareness stage for school administrators. At the local level, the test of educational leaders is to develop the leadership of parents, community members, and most of all, students. Such leaders may develop a vision beyond the immediate situation and connections with broader movements in their own society as well as others. Leadership, which evolves as a significant factor in large-scale movements, is discussed in Chapter 4.

Leaders reach across national borders and develop international visions, but such visions are always rooted in individual situations. The immediate situations involve students that leaders in education must bring with them if their visions are to be realized. New technology and progressive education, such as in the Galileo project, attracts administrators who are concerned with the learning of students. Students are either instructing teachers about the technology or giving them important reasons to become more technologically literate. Similarly, in such a context administrators are aware of how much they as professionals, can learn from the new professions linked to computers.

In schools with such leaders, students will emerge larger than their expected roles in schools. Student leaders will gain the momentum to move towards the international stage. The Galileo has students connecting with professionals constructing space ships (Jacobsen & Gladstone, 2002). Through technological connections, students are asking artists about their constructions (Mitchell 2000a). Distant tutors are becoming more possible in a variety of mediums. The infrastructure to make broader connections possible needs to be created by partnerships.

Chapter 4
Social Movements

Once in Chelm, the mythical village of the East European Jews, a man was appointed to sit at the village gate and wait for the coming of the Messiah. He complained to the village elders that his pay was too low. "You are right," they said to him, "the pay is low. But consider: the work is steady." (Quoted in Elmore & McLaughlin, 1998, p. 1)

Business, government, and community agencies are redrawing the line between public and private spheres as they form partnerships with schools. Partnerships are part of global change linking private companies, voluntary organizations, and schools (Pal, 2001). As a result of these changes in thinking about partnerships, groups within society play active roles within schools, while school personnel join community projects.

All relationships in society are involved in new forms of partnerships. Until recently in the United States, schools ignored religion despite the fact that churches were their oldest partner. Currently, alliances between schools and religious groups are supported and publicized. Religion could provide richer experiences for education than is acknowledged. Symbolic and ritualistic links provide people with multiple meanings and myths to enhance spiritual support for participation in partnerships.

Only in isolated cases is it possible to find religious imagery and ritual in programs of partnerships. Celebrations of successful partnerships in communities are the main event in which rituals are introduced. Successes become significant when they involve at-risk students, whether the project relates to artists, businesses, scientists, or community service partners. These organizations have a common aim to provide services for children or young adults in the greatest need. Creative leaders can create multiple partnerships when visions and resources are shared.

Multiple partners may amalgamate the perspectives of separate partners for the benefit of individual students. Sharing information and common procedures are major problems in developing integration of partners. A large number of partners allow schools to change. Increasing the resources of schools may mean that parallel organizations occasionally complement each other. In an age of partnerships, cooperation may develop in different directions to create a variety of schools.

FOUNDATIONS

The creation of new schools or alternative projects within existing schools is the aim of many foundation grants. The gift givers are a new link between business, schools, and voluntary organizations. In the United States, reform movements have become dependent on them (Mitchell, 1996). For example, in Chicago, a coordinated campaign of donors provided $100 million to change agents over five years (McKersie, 1993).

Plans for arts education and social services integration were torpedoed by the decisions of foundations (Sommerfeld, 1994; Mitchell, 2000a). The paper chase for funding makes partnership projects dependent on foundations. The fourth largest American foundation, the Pew Charitable Trust, announced a major commitment to the integration of social services for $60 million over ten years, but changed its position after two years, limiting its allocations to a total of $8 million (Sommerfeld, 1994). The Pew grants initiated a network of family centres, and the state of Kentucky spent an estimated $1 million of staff time in planning for them. Kentucky and other states turned to the Annie B. Casey Foundation and the Foundation for Child Development for support to integrate social services. The Pew Foundation made a similar pledge to arts education for five years; it cancelled this offer after one year, leaving the partners in disarray (Mitchell, 2000a).

If they cannot make schools and their partners dependent upon them, the foundations become critics or partners in the process of change themselves. In Pittsburgh, the Heinz Endowments, Pittsburgh Foundation, and the Grable Foundation cancelled $3 million in grants a year because of "bickering, distrust, and chaotic decision making" by the public schools (Associated Press, 2002). Foundations created by companies are the main sources of corporate involvement in schools (S. Reid, presentation, April 9, 2000). Company foundations are able to sponsor many projects that the diverse partners of community foundations would probably not agree upon. In 2003, the Calgary Board of Education formed its own foundation to raise more money than it could obtain from foundations.

The Panasonic Foundation is an active player in the process of innovation and the campaign for educational reform. After being started by the electronic giant Matsushita, it transformed itself into a consulting firm for individual schools and departments of education that have not attempted any reforms (Mitchell, 1996). This unique company foundation has created tensions among educators. In Santa Fe, New Mexico, for example, the foundation ignored conflicts between central office and principals, and between administrators and teachers. Although there is evidence of changed teachers and school practices, several of the original Panasonic partnerships are defunct. In spite of its problems Panasonic continues to be active; it is doing what other foundations would like to do. However, other foundations are not trying to change schools so directly.

The goals of foundations and the organizations they sponsor become active in times of crises or when educational reform becomes a social movement. The individual Chicago foundations started to speak of themselves as agents for social change. These foundations hire community activists and support reform principles. The power of volunteers and their advocates is being both increased and directed by foundations, primarily through the training of the new school councils (McKersie, 1993). After reform legislation was enacted, the foundations increased their support to community groups nearly threefold.

In Chicago, the foundation personnel are 'likeminded' people who became more progressive after the arrival of Peter Martinez with the MacArthur Foundation, one of the largest foundations in America (William McKersie, interview, November 2, 1993). Mr. Martinez was an organizer for over twenty years with the radical organization founded by Saul Alinsky. He saw the potentialities of building on the base that Alinsky created in Chicago as well as the talents of current educators and social activists.

Nationally, the more neutral organization, the Pew Forum, which is supported by the Pew Foundation, urged California foundations to be far more active in educational reform (Mitchell, 1996). For many people the image of foundations is like a conservative comptroller (Mitchell, 2000a). The foundations not only become socially active during crises, they follow fads at other times; partnerships are a pet cause (Community Foundations of Canada, 2001). During the 1930s, foundations supported the integration of social services and schools; they abandoned the cause because of a concern for a lack of scientific evidence for projects they supported and, fifty years later, have come back to service integration although there is still no rigorous proof of its effectiveness (Mitchell, 1996).

Nationally, a chain of executives with foundations was linked in the 1990s because they knew each other as social activists in the 1960s. In Chicago, as well as in other cities, a core group of foundation executives began working together as college students in the National Coalition of Advocates for Students, and were still involved as foundation executives in the National Coalition of Education Activists (Ann Hallett, interview, October 25, 1993). The five or six executives for foundations in this group were on the brink of becoming political radicals.

Interest in foundations is spreading across America and the world. In the United States, the total reform of the educational system in Kentucky is supported by every possible foundation and government source. The Kellogg Foundation supports reforms in the education of health workers in many countries (Mitchell, 2002). The Aga Khan and Asia Foundations are major forces in Asia as well as other countries (Mitchell, Klinck & Burger, 2004). Although the United States relies on foundations and companies to support innovations, other countries, such as Canada, rely on government support. However, these countries are turning to foundations (D. Thornburn, presentation, July 29, 2002). In Australia, the Education Foundation has become an active partner that engages companies and, in turn, actively supports school reforms with the money and personnel from businesses (Black, 2004).

There are direct links between foundations in the United States and events elsewhere. An immigrant from the United States, Ellen Koshland. modeled the Australian foundation that she founded on one in San Francisco (Black, 2004). The Chicago developments were brought to Canada by John McKnight whose ideas influence community foundations north of the American border (Canadian Broadcasting Corporation, 1994; Community Foundations of Canada, 2001). Foundations in each of these countries support reform that promises to increase community and parental involvement. The innovation of integrated social services is a result of these community directions.

As they become involved in social movements for reform, foundations become as politically active as the law allows. At the time of Chicago reform, an executive with the Joyce Foundation, William McKersie, said he would fight his own board to get support for school reform (Mitchell, 1996). As a group, the foundations considered, but would not endorse, legislative proposals for changing school governance because of the possible loss of their nonprofit tax status if they were seen to be lobbying (William McKersie, interview, November 2, 1993). Twenty-one funders signed a letter urging adoption of reform principles, principles that corresponded to the legislation that was adopted.

In contrast, Canada's legislation forbids any grants for advocacy. A foundation can give money to support food banks, but cannot contribute to efforts to found such banks! In Alberta, Canada, a number of foundations supported research, conferences, and publicity on charter schools (Mitchell, 2001c). The opposition of trustees, unions, and administrators is so substantial that charter schools might not have developed without this support. John McCarthy, then Director of the Canadian Charter School Centre, reports possible speakers from the established organizations in education declined to speak on the subject of charters (Personal communication, February, 1999).

In different countries, foundation support brings universities into the arena of educational change where they, in turn, may become active partners. Partnerships are a means for universities to be involved in developing social policies. In the American South the historic black colleges, are being recruited along with universities to be partners for schools (Sansbury, 2004). The Kellogg Foundation in United States, South Africa, and other countries develops an integration of health services and the training of health professionals in rural areas (Mitchell, 2002). Although they have used local schools for training, the Kellogg Foundation's primary links for health education are with universities.

Universities are brought into educational reform to legitimate the changes. In Chicago, after foundations increased their funding for community groups, universities became a part of reforming education (Mitchell, 1996). Before the reform legislation or any action by foundations, Dan Lewis made a study of school decentralization which became the basis for a citywide conference (McKerzie, 1993; Lewis & Nakagawa, 1995). At that time, there were few other research studies or regular academic groups involved in reform. After the reforms were introduced and increased foundation activity came to support the reformers' efforts, a host of academic groups began providing their services as well as preparing research as a part of a consortium. By 1990, major grants were made to universities as well as to reform groups.

Foundations lag behind changes, although not as much as universities. They are more attuned to business and political changes than academics may want to be. Radical critics of foundations explain the action of foundations as a way of disguising the conservative power of large corporations (Knowles, 1973). Historical analyses of foundations show conservative positions, including racial segregation, are promoted by educational reports that foundations supported in the United States and abroad(Berman, 1989).

Neutral interpreters of foundations stress the separation of foundations from corporations and indicate the political knowledge that foundation executives possess allows them to set the agenda for reform policy (Lagemann, 1989). The lag between social groups and support by foundations would indicate lack of knowledge and understanding rather than bias.

When researchers become committed to reforms, their knowledge becomes suspect. Studies of Chicago reforms show that democratic school councils are the basis for effective reforms and school-based management (Mitchell, 1996). This evidence for democratic councils is linked to particular ethnic and racial groups involved in the councils. Latinos, rather than Blacks, account for most of the open and democratic councils. The study shows that Latinos are similar to the Irish in that they excel in political skills.

The Consortium on Chicago School Research includes all universities in the Chicago area and does most of the research on Chicago education; its dominant position limits discussion of Chicago reform because outsiders are not given the same resources and recognition. Explanations are sought by those with the Consortium when test results are unfavourable for reform, but they expect there to be improvements. One independent professor says, "he fix is in for reform in Chicago" (Dan Lewis, interview, October 25, 1993).

Foundations must show results in education or what looks like results. In Chicago, the initial lack of test score increases by Chicago's students put pressure on foundation executives to justify their investment. The MacArthur Foundation responded by emphasizing conventional projects, such as standard setting, rather than community organizing. (Peter Martinez, interview, April 25, 1994). If there are no tangible results, foundations look to justification by the procedures they use. Similar foundation actions are found in South Africa, Australia, and Pakistan to create professional forums as well as rigourous methods (Mitchell, Klinck & Burger, 2004).

RELIGION

Justifying their faith in education by research or procedures suggests a link to religious thinking. However, the link among foundations, community action, and religion is not obvious. Several members of the clergy were on the Chicago School

Board. The Methodist organization, Child-Save is a member of the Citizens Schools Committee. The Reverend Kenneth Smith, a professor at the Chicago School of Theology, and an advisor to Mayor Daley's assemblies for reform and the Citizens Schools Committee, says the school reform movement had no religious images or moral aims (Interview, October 21, 1993).

Smith tellingly notes that the City Missionary Society changed its name to the Community Renewal Society. The Community Renewal Society is the sponsor of Chicago's journal of reform, *Catalyst*. Four foundations came together to support the founding of Catalyst, in a common commitment, because of the substantial funding required (Mitchell, 1996). *Catalyst* hardly reveals any link to the Community Renewal Society and none to its predecessor. It pretends to be an independent paper.

In Chicago and similar cities, there are other links to religion. Fred Hess, who holds a Divinity Degree and was Executive Director of the Chicago Panel On School Policy when legislation for reform passed, notes that the United Church of Christ remains a sponsor of important organizations, including his own. (Fred Hess, interview, November 15, 1993). Individual churches are recruiting grounds for accountants who want to be involved in school-based management (Mitchell, 1996). In another Midwest city, true believers in educational reform were involved in a series of movements and a variety of innovations (Smith et al., 1986). In other countries, the historical religions continue to affect the way in-service education is delivered (Molyneux and Wooley, 2004). In Vietnam, Australian progressive educators had to overcome an authoritarian influence that can be traced back to Confucius.

Integrated services reveal disguised religious links to school services; they avoid direct ties to religious leaders. In Bracken County, Kentucky, the high school has the ten commandments on its steps and religious leaders are invited as assembly speakers, but there is no link to the family resource centre on the same site (Judith Toomey, interview, May 5, 1995). Similarly, although Black ministers are a mainstay of the community, an extensive program of integrated services in the Orr

High School of Chicago has no religious leaders involved. In a number of communities, such as Calgary, Canada, councils of churches acted as sponsors for these service projects (Mitchell, 1996).

The relationship between churches and schools remains behind a curtain, which is starting to lift. In Kentucky, Susan Schweder, a coordinator of family resource centres in Lexington, said that, if their funding was cut, they would turn to the churches for help (Interview, May 8, 1995). Similar responses were found in Chicago and Alberta, Canada (Mitchell, 1996). However, right-wing religious and political leaders attack family resource centers; in Kentucky they suggested that these centers were "Nazi child snatchers" (Marcia Morganti, interview, May 5, 1995).

The administration of George W. Bush offers federal support to religious groups to provide social services (Davis, 2002). Those who oppose involving church groups object to such groups being called "partners" since the term suggests a union of church and state (Freethought, 2000). Again, it is the extreme right that objects to this invasion of individual rights.

In the United States, radical community groups combine religion with community organization as the basis for their school reform efforts. The Industrial Areas Foundation (IAF) by Saul Alinksy was, from its inception, allied with the Catholic church, but today is involved with diverse religious groups, including Muslems (Mitchell, 1996). The leader of the Texas affiliate of IAF, Ernesto Cortes, was a key figure, along with Ross Perot, in securing educational reform and received a "genius" award from the MacArthur Foundation for this and other social action efforts. Cortes involves conservative religious groups in East Texas, such as the Church of Christ, with his community action projects and league of schools.

The influence of the IAF is resisted by the reformers who want to cooperate with the establishment (Mitchell, 1996). In Chicago, leaders of neighborhood organizations, such as Danny Soltis with United Neighborhood Organization, maintain their independence from the IAF. Coretta McFerren, a key member of the Chicago reform coalitions, says she had to "deprogram herself" from Alinsky methods, which include direct confrontation (Corretta McFerren, interview, October 26, 1993). In Seattle, Greg Tuke, Executive Director of Powerful Schools, was trained in a similar approach to that of Alinsky, but he now works from an office in an elementary school to improve the schools' curriculum and parent involvement (Mitchell, 2000a). The activists for education move away from the combination of labour movement methods and religious proselytizing that characterized their origins.

Moderate religious involvement with schools is accepted and is the tradition of many societies and cultures. For example, in Canada, the parish and publicly supported Catholic schools are related through the work of the priest and parents. Core groups are able to reach supporters and find funds for a variety of projects. The former arts coordinator for the Calgary Catholic Board, Lorraine Kneier, speaks of a group that organized to raise funds for band instruments (Personal communication, March, 1999). Because of its diversity in terms of business and professional links, this group is able to raise funds for any project. The instruments are now provided by the government. When developed, personal contacts make the union of church and schools powerful. These opportunities are missed by those who strive to avoid religion.

Aside from developing contacts and providing social services, the emphasis and understanding of religious groups is generally unappreciated. For example, the environmental movement needs to emphasize the groves and places that previous generations believed were 'set apart' (Mountain Institute, 1998). Sacred sites are not preserved unless their origin is an archeological mystery. The National Religious Partnerships include the U.S. Catholic Conference, National Council of Churches of Christ, Coalition on the Environment and Jewish Life, and the Evangelical Environmental Network (DiPeso, n.d.). The latter group works with a secular organization to publish *Creation Care* to raise awareness about the environment from a Biblical perspective. There are dramatic examples such as the "Redwood Rabbis" who stop the clear-cutting of old-growth forests.

Removing the blinders from the principles of partnerships concerning religion affects related movements for change. The environmental movement is an ally for arts education (Mitchell, 2000a) while the arts and religion are intertwined. Religion and the arts are both effective sources for preventing drug addition and repeat criminal offenses among young offenders (Office of National Drug Control Policy, 2001; Mitchell, 2000b).

There are effective sources for helping students that derive from religion. The value of celebrations for developing partnerships is proclaimed, but the value of other rituals is ignored. Studies of ritual and ceremonies by anthropologists or post-modern writers on religion are not considered. The founders of partnerships follow modern thinkers and ignore religion and are surprised if outside research suggests it is significant (Diana Lauber, interview, April 11, 1993).

There are exceptions, particularly among Natives. At Fox Lake in Northern Canada, Cree art and beliefs are brought together with Catholic religion (Short, 1998). The Virgin Mary is depicted on a drum for the "Dance of the Ancestors" while the Catholic priest, Father Paul Hernou, learns to refer to Jesus as "Our Elder Brother" (Ibid, p. 99). Paintings at the Catholic Church show the same integration of previously separate traditions. Ritual and arts contain rich possibilities for school partnerships. There are other exceptions and combinations of religions, such as in North Carolina, where a Jewish synagogue and a Muslim mosque both became partners with a local school (North Carolina Council of Churches, 2002).

A barometer of acceptance for religious partnerships is the support provided by foundations (Pew Charitable Trusts, 2001). The Pew Foundation has a grant program called *Religion and Social Welfare Policy Strategy* to consider the "constitutional issues" and "effectiveness of faith-based social services." A Philadelphia program and a proposed national project for at-risk youth are seen as critical for such "cross-sector partnerships." The hedging of language by the Director of the Pew project, Luis Lugo, suggests the limits of efforts for anti-risk students, in general, and Hispanic ones, in particular.

More radical ideas concerning religion and social change were spread by the followers of Saul Alinsky and his writings. His ideas are spread by Frontier College in Canada to Natives and those fighting poverty. The same reserve at Fox Lake where art and religion are developed is the site from which radicalization of local efforts emerges. The question is whether this site, or others like it, will provide effective examples of programs for First Nation students whose alienation produces suicide rates twice that of the average for Canadians (Short, 1999).

Religious ties with schools for Aboriginals is an example which is ignored by other groups. In the Plains Indian school in Calgary, Canada, religion is included in the First Nation program (Mitchell, 1990); the school is the only one in the public system that teaches religion, although this has not led to open criticism. The Natives are simply viewed as an exception. Other groups will have to discover the potential of religious partnerships by themselves.

GLOBALIZATION

Aboriginal peoples and other minorities show some of the differences that remain among ethnic and racial groups within one country. The differences between American and European partnerships show how resilient other cultural differences are to globalization (Pal, 2000). Many cultures resist these tendencies, but decline in the number of languages and daily differences in lives suggests how powerful is the tendency to centralization.

Partnerships that spread to different countries are modified in varying degrees. Those that integrate the functions of partners in a common organization are the slowest to spread (Mitchell, 1998). The Coalition of Essential Schools (CES) is the largest single reform organization. CES has a base at Brown University, partnership with ten states, and a few affiliates in Canada (Mitchell, 1998). In contrast, the National Writing Project has spread to include a variety of affiliates in Canada, Europe, and five Commonwealth Countries. The National Writing Project requires local coordinators, a summer workshop, and interested people to create a program that involves different interpretations by separate individuals.

The question is whether the ideas of the organization spread when the organization does not. Canadians live next to a giant, and educational reform follows the steps made by Americans; however Canadians resist joining American organizations (Mitchell, 2002). The ideas of CES spread to many school boards, including Edmonton. Ted Sizer, the founder of CES, advised the Galileo technology partnership in Calgary when it was attacked, to go forth and multiply (Mitchell, 2002).

The issue of organizational affiliation is crystallized by the philosophy of Saul Alinsky who founded the IAF (Mitchell, 1996; Mitchell, 1998). Although there are affiliates in many American cities as well as England, Alinsky believed in no permanent affiliates. An annual contract is renewed each year so that the organizations, like individuals, would not become subordinate. The national organization would undertake any task that the affiliates could do by themselves. Former affiliates and individuals trained by Alinsky showed their independence in resisting the return of IAF to its original home in Chicago. The work with Aboriginal people in Canada represented diffusion of ideas, rather than organizational affiliates.

Although globalization stresses the indirect effects of modeling and imitation, direct efforts to link voluntary organizations internationally are limited. The American unification of voluntary organizations as the independent sector, under the initial leadership of Brian O'Connell, is an example of international affiliation. John Gardner, an O'Connell advisor, provided leadership ideas which have spread even further than O'Connell's organization (O'Connell. 1998; Gardner, 1990). In the last chapter, Gardner's work with student leaders was traced in communities near his Standford center.

This unity of voluntary organizations of the independent sector affects lobbying, research, and status for national organizations. The need for recognition leads has resulted the organization of the International Society for Third-Sector Research. This federation is removed from the work of local volunteers and was dominantly influenced in its formation by national mental health organizations.

Affiliation is significant when it promotes the formation of local groups. The citizens' advocacy group, Common Cause, which promotes town-meeting discussions, was founded by John Gardner. Gardner also started Civics, the World Alliance for Citizen Participation, which tries to reach across borders. Similar organizations in different countries are affiliated, but linking local organizations in a meaningful way to individual members is difficult.

Communities in Schools (CIS) is a program that retains local roots while spreading internationally. CIS accepts modification between countries as it does variations within the United States. Beginning in 1994, CIS initiated international programs in England and Canada (Mitchell, 1996; Communities in Schools, 2001). The British program, "CIS Bridge Course," is an independent organization based upon the American model. The British course concentrates on no more than ten students who are attending a Further Education College or Adult Education Centre. Groups in Ireland and Northern Ireland organized with the assistance from the American organization and its Canadian leader, Janet Longmore.

The Canadian group is linked to the American parent. In 1995, CIS formed a national organization in Canada based on projects in Toronto and Yorkton, Saskatchewan (Mitchell, 1998). CIS established a program for six sites in Atlantic Canada. This program focuses on topics, such as private sector investment or transition from school to work. The Atlantic project is supported by a grant from the Atlantic Canada Opportunities Agency. The program reflects the emphasis of the top business leaders in Canada, who do not believe in education as a faith like those in the United States. Government grants rather than business donations keeps CIS involved in Canada. In Ontario, the Trillium Foundation, a foundation created by the government of Ontario, provided a grant for evaluation of CIS.

The argument for globalization is that international organizations become alike (Pal, 2001). When English organizations are affiliated, they are different and remain independent. Canadian groups either do not affiliate or, in the case of CIS, reflect Canadians interests in economic improvement. A variation of the globalization argument says organizations do not necessarily become more alike, but they become more aware of similar organizations in other countries. Students in Australia and Canada become aware of their different holidays and seasons, when they are in the same internet course (Stacey & Wiesenberg, 2004). This argument also fits Australian experience when foundations evolve from an American model (Black, 2004). Rural and religious groups are most distinctive and usually oppose modern ideas, such as the education of girls in Pakistan (Rizvi and Sayeed, 2004). Opposition to globalization by religious groups is highly publicized, but quality teacher education and professional efforts are believed to be able to create networks to overcome these local opponents (Wheeler & Pardham, 2004) .

MULTIPLE PARTNERS

International relationships are an extension of multiple efforts at the local level. Three or more partners may bring people, resources and ideas together that dual partnerships cannot match. In addition to these ingredients, triple relationships generate publicity and awards that not only celebrate success, but also generate future support from all stakeholders, including foundations.

In South Carolina, several partners complement each other in an arts partnership (Mitchell, 2000a). The state department of education has a larger budget than the arts agency, but lacks the legitimacy of the state arts department. The university is capable of bringing these and other organizations together in the ABC alliance for the arts. Although this program influences similar developments in Oklahoma and Mississippi, it cannot be copied without its complex relationships.

Multiple partnerships do create greater social distance between teachers and partnerships. The classroom rather than the school is the reality for teachers, but the plan for education and the community goes beyond the school. Although schools are linked into networks, such networks often only relate schools to school districts (Sirotnik & Goodlad, 1988). Europeans have a longer history of involving the outside world while maintaining the autonomy of the schools. Cross-sector planning in Europe begins at the national level. Unlike European practice, for North Americans distant governments provide only signals to schools about change, not conferences for directions (Goertz, 2001).

At a local level, American boards weigh the aims of new partnerships, but fail to review the accomplishments of established ones (Mitchell, 2002). Such a review is needed if partnerships are to be expanded. Exclusive franchises for one partner company always raise questions because they eliminate options. Dual or multiple partnerships expand the resources, ideas, and people that can be connected to schools.

Another way to evaluate partnerships is to eliminate all of them at a set time unless adopted again "sunset legislation." Some states, such as Colorado, eliminate all governmental rules and regulations, unless enacted again under 'sunset legislation. Old partnerships could receive the same treatment in order not to take gifts for granted and make partners prove added value. In order to discover new options, partners can be creative and suggest new policies for themselves and their allies. Creative solutions require a merging of options (Follett, 1973). Partners should be contributors to schools in the same way that businesspeople become involved in the process of contributing to the arts when they engage in related activities such as performing or creating scenery (Mitchell, 2000a). Just as the industrial revolution did not occur in the country with the most gold, schools need people and ideas to achieve excellence.

Aside from the external partners, multiplying influence of any part of the educational system requires changes in the other levels from early childhood education to graduate school. If the struggles between universities and schools can be put aside, common goals defined, and the interests of the two parties respected, significant partnerships involving these parties will develop. The universities are able to influence many other parties, including the mass media, technologists, and lawyers to form partnerships. Schools, with the help of universities, are capable of assembling a powerful chorus of parents, teachers, and students for the partnership drama, such as G.W. University. Georgia has announced an extensive program of colleges and universities assisting schools with disadvantaged students (Sansbury, 2004). In

Pakistan, the Aga Khan Foundation formed an Institute of Education together with Oxford University, the University of Toronto, and consultants from other world-class universities (Wheeler and Pardham, 2004).

Another strategic set of partners in various countries are lawyers and politicians because they are in a position to encourage other businesspeople, professionals, and perhaps, university officials to support schools and engage in dialogue. The Galileo project in Alberta, Canada, has two law firms representing it in an attempt to combine technological change with student-centred education (Mitchell, 2002). Lawyers help bring organized projects into existence by drafting the articles of incorporation. They are involved with top-level meetings of governors or ministers of education as well as business leaders, and develop links for continuing local partnerships. Politicians are able to mobilize community support, celebrations of success, and legislative grants (Mitchell, 2000a).

Although claiming to be above the crowd, foundations are influenced by it, as illustrated by the events in Chicago reform. Foundations are interested in showing how their grants multiply their effects. If possible, foundations want to see their grants matched, three or four times. In North Carolina, The Kenan Institute lobbies state legislatures to match its own grants while persuading other foundations and business groups to match their grants several times over (Mitchell, 2000a). Some businesses, such as Shell Oil in Los Angeles, attempt to stimulate other businesses as local partners (Clearinghouse of Educational Management, n.d.).

Multiple links among key partners are being created. Foundations and governments try to connect universities to schools (Mitchell, 1998). Businesses provide support to universities but they increasingly monitor their research and expect to be involved in the education of its executives and professionals (Mitchell, 1996). Professional development schools are one of the links between schools and higher education. Professional development schools make schools a partner in teacher training, action research, and professional development; in a few cases they go even further to improve health and social services in schools (Mitchell, 1998: Mitchell, 2002). The

Coalition of Essential Schools (CES) has a university base at Brown University, while the Galileo project in Alberta, Canada, housed on the campus of the University of Calgary, is supported by the other Alberta universities.

Universities, technical schools, and community colleges are important partners because they all have educational aims. American businesses are amateurs in education, but European businesses, including German engineering firms operating in the United States and Canada, are experienced in education for the skilled trades (Mitchell, 2002). On both sides of the Atlantic, businesses and schools converge when their joint staffs are in the same technological training program.

Similarly, teachers and parents who learn about community development and the arts together become an effective advocacy group for schools, such as in Mississippi where a professional organization for the arts works closely with a parent group that promotes community forums (Mitchell, 2000a). Professional development programs for teachers are increasingly including community leaders (National Association for Promotion of Partnerships, 2001). The key question is the extent to which such partners are involved in a common mission.

Businesses and other institutions are just discovering common themes in their education programs, such as the importance of learning circles as well as other key ideas for education (Nelson & Zadek, 2000). Universities, through leagues with schools, had made the same discovery many years prior to this (Mitchell, 1998). Universities exist to understand and spread an understanding of multiple and long-term goals. In Pakistan, local university faculty resist the influence of professors from Oxford and the University of Toronto (Wheeler & Pardham, 2004). The vision of local faculty may be more concerned with the particular purposes of schools.

Within the universities, faculties of education can be exemplars of effective partnerships, just as when they developed school leagues and associations. Education students are capable of working with virtual schools to train adults in basic skills, serve in communities, participate in business-schools links, or become participants in arts partnerships. As active contributors rather than guests in schools, they would provide valuable assistance to these projects and communities.

The Human Resource Program at George Washington University suggests how much education and other students could contribute to schools and communities. Differences among teachers, such as those in special education and regular classes, can be overcome in the training of teachers for each area (Mitchell, 1990). Teachers in special education in a few universities, such as the University of Washington, are part of multiple training in related professions (Mitchell, 1992).

New problems provide a basis for universities and schools to put aside old feuds. The W. W. Kellogg Foundation sees the preparation of health professionals for rural communities as a new goal for universities and community agencies (Mitchell, 2002). Although it enhances the effectiveness of rural schools, technology is a general means to increase cooperation between universities, schools, and communities (Foote, et al., 1999).

Technology spawns networks and partnerships for adults and children. In format, these are either progressive or highly structured. If they are innovative in either direction, schools or community projects attract technologists. Education students have opportunities to develop webs, show teachers and others how technology improves their lives, and act as catalysts or consultants in the new economy. Students should be involved in a variety of specific projects across boundaries.

PLANNING BY AN ELITE

Technological change, universities, and globalization may lead to a preoccupation with planning for a small group that claims to have benefits for others. For example a visiting teacher program is thought to have a multiplier effect so that 1170 teacher graduates could influence 175,500 students (Wheeler & Pardhan, 2004, pp. 142-143). That there would be resistance in an underdeveloped country to modernization guided by an elite is not included in this calculation. The authors note that local faculty with universities resist international colleagues who are dominant. They do not carry this argument further although they are writing about a country where traditional religious schools and religious extremists are strongly supported.

Extreme positions in planning often lead to exactly the opposite results from what is intended. Village schools supported by NGOs aim to extend education to girls, but will the schools are better than government ones and there are fears about the safety of girls, these schools are chosen for boys by their parents (Rizvi & Sayeed, 2004). Quality education involving Western universities can make the education of various 'have-nots' worse in poor countries.

The preoccupation with professionals administering elite or international education is with working with people like themselves. In Pakistan, the Aga Khan Institute founded by Oxford and University of Toronto leads to creation of various councils and forums to coordinate their efforts, but no effort to reach people who are excluded by income or social origins from entering teacher education. Similarly, there is a profusion of professional organizations that have resulted from this institute's emphasis on academic specialists. Saul Alinsky would act very differently.

THE ORR NETWORK

In Chicago, where Alinsky started, there has been in at least one case of development of excessive partnership relationships. For the Rezin Orr Academy High School in Chicago, there is a question of focus. The Orr Network is stretching the limit of possible partners within the school and between the school and community agencies. Twelve elementary and middle schools combine with the Orr High School on the northwestern side of Chicago in a host of varied activities.

The Orr Network exists in a community characterized by Black poverty, young people who have young children, and a population that has abandoned hope. Seventy-five percent of the community is below the poverty line, and the average age is twenty-five (Bill Duffie, interview, May 11, 1995). Several of the feeder schools are mainly Latino. The high school wants more students to enroll from the elementary schools in the network, while the feeder schools seek services from the high school to which they are linked. (Mitchell, 1996). This network is in a community, like others in Chicago, where only the church, school, and liquor store remain after businesses and professional services leave (Coretta McFerren, interview, May 5,

1994).

In such a community, out of desperation, many educational and social changes are attempted aside from the Orr Network. Staff training for teachers is provided through a system-wide initiative, Creating A New Approach to Learning (CANAL). CANAL involves learning school-based management within a conflict situation (Mitchell, 1996). Other school projects include a variation of the Great Books program, Paideia. The Orr school received a grant from the foundation founded by Bill Gates that was made to small schools (Diana Lauber, email, July 19, 2000). The Orr high school is also creating a junior military training school. The most important partnership for parents has long been one that makes the children's trip to and from school safe. The safety program is part of Broader Urban Involvement and Leadership Development (BUILD). BUILD organizes parent patrols to protect students from gangs and drugs.

CIS brought social services to the schools before the Orr Network was organized; they expanded after its inception. The high school operates the Ounce of Prevention, a school health clinic, which has not been incorporated into the Orr Network (Bill Staughton, interview, May 11, 1995). This is one of the high school's programs not shared with the feeder schools because they were established before the network. The health clinic at the Ryerson Elementary School, unlike the one at the Orr High School, is open to the community (Mitchell, 1996). Neither the high school, the feeder schools, nor community organizations have negotiated to include programs, such as the Ounce of Prevention, into the Orr Network. In addition to the two health centers, there are two family centers, the Nia Family Center in the community, and one in the high school. The Nia Family Center provides early childhood education together with health services, while the high school program is focused on young parents who also have a daycare facility in the school (Mitchell, 1996).

The irony of these and other problems in relating school and community partnership is that there is a Development Council for this purpose. The Nia Family Center was developed by the West Humboldt Park Family and Community Development Council. This council extends the Orr project into planning libraries, parks and prospective businesses. The Orr Network itself maintains an employment center and a base for community development. Orr's Development Council increases changes in the community. Community concerns include local employment, libraries, and health clinics (Mitchell, 1996). In 1992, a planning agency was established to relate the diverse areas of policing gangs, health services, affordable housing, and business opportunities to the needs of people. Opportunities for young people depend on this project for basic and adult education. However, the Orr project's Development Council no longer provides job opportunities for high school graduates (Bill Duffie & Bill Staughton, interviews, May 11, 1995).

Outsiders as a planning group encounter many problems. The Bank of America claims an exclusive franchise as company sponsor that makes the school and community dependent on it. The Orr network was created by outsiders including those from the Continental Bank (Nancy Brandt, interviews, November 2, 1993 and May 11, 1995). Nancy Brandt, the bank sponsor, Barbara Radner, DePaul University educator, and Ann Greenwood from the oldest arts education program in Chicago, ART, provided coordination and continuity for the Orr project (Nancy Brandt, interview, November, 1993). The departure of Ann Greenwood has never been overcome.

Active arts programs were developed in the network schools through the help of the Chicago Arts Partnership in Education (CAPE). The art program for the Orr Network was to integrate the arts with other curriculum areas, such as English; one elementary school, Noble, was a model of arts-centred teaching for all subjects. After one year, CAPE dropped the Orr High School from its foundation sponsored activities because it had so many partnerships that arts education was not receiving its due efforts – the program at Nobel is an important exception (A. Aprill, personal communication, November, 2001).

The DePaul University's Center for Urban Education continues to provide a resource coordinator who works with both the arts and science curriculums (Barbara Radner, interview, November 11, 1993). DePaul obtained funds for many of the other Orr Network projects, including a writing program and one in contextual mathematics, together with specialists in each case. DePaul also helps find and train parent and teacher volunteers. Former Peace Corps members, as well as newer student volunteers, work as teaching assistants; DePaul includes the Orr schools in this network. Training programs for parents are centred on the basic curriculum. A parent coordinator works with a community representative from each of the Orr schools. Parent rooms are located in each of the schools, and the high school has a family resource centre.

For both parents and staff, curriculum variety is important (Mitchell, 1996). The Golden Apple Foundation brings 'hands-on' science and materials to network schools as well as giving awards to excellent teachers. There are many partners for curriculum projects that continue (Mitchell, 1996). These contributors include the Shedd Aquarium, which provides staff training, special nights for all Orr parents, and programs at the aquarium for students. On-line technical assistance is available from the Teachers' Academy for Mathematics and Science. The Children's Museum provides a family science program, while the Max McGraw Wildlife Foundation offers staff development on animals and conservation. The Orr High School helps elementary schools establish after-school science programs and operates a store where they are able to purchase science materials.

The arts program still involves almost as many partners as those in the science area. Students continue to participate in the Marwen gallery's program of studio training where they prepared a large mural for the Orr High School. For the Marwen art gallery program, which provides professional apprenticeships, students are bused from elementary schools to the studios by high school buses. The high school was the scene of two special performances of *Die Fliedermaus*, by the Lyric Opera. Dance companies present programs for the schools as a part of regular classes. The Orr High School has difficulty coordinating so many programs (Bill Duffie, interview, May 11, 1995).

The success of the Orr partnerships depended on the involvement of individuals and a group of sponsors. The Orr Network is meaningful for those involved in its informal planning and parent groups. For teachers and students, the project is fragmented; a math teacher uses its math program as a resource (Bill Duffie, interview, May 11, 1995). The separation of the nursery from the rest of the high schools by double-locked doors must convey a message to teen parents. Questions are also raised by staff who resist the increasing number of non-academic tasks that are asked to assume. The limitations of the Orr project cannot be hidden from students (Bill Slaughton, interview, May 11, 1995). The expansion of the project exposes the limitation of the school, the community council's concern for education, and the difficulties of maintaining a planning group.

TOWARDS A FEDERATED SYSTEM OF COORDINATION

Problems of a local site assuming as many tasks as the Orr Network may be resolved by a two-level system of coordination. A two-tier system of governance for partnerships allows the members to deal with two separate problems, management and survival (North Central Regional Educational Laboratory, n.d.). For managerial efficiency, the smaller group allows for an immediate response to demands while a large group focuses on long-term issues. Similar to the Orr Project, the Local Investment Commission in Kansas City, Missouri, is a consortium to provide neighbourhood services. A professional cabinet of experts advises the 36-member of business executives and low income parents on professional development and social services. Three permanent committees cover financial operations, evaluation, and publicity.

Kentucky provides an example of a managerial function, coordinating diverse partnerships that requires consensus among principals, teachers, and parents. The Kentucky Association of School Councils was formed in 1991 when David Allen of the Kentucky Education Association (the teachers' union) and Jean Arrowwood of the Kentucky Congress of Parents and Teachers convened a meeting of the three constituencies. Training, legal services, publications, and an annual convention are provided by this association of councils. In Kentucky, a lawyer, writer on reform and former associate with the U.S. Department of Education, Susan Weston, was hired as the first executive director. Without grass-roots support, Kentucky pursues an elaborate attempt to train and involve passive parents.

For political survival, the separation of levels works differently. Continuity is maintained by a small group expanding and replacing itself over time while the larger group mobilizes to resist deadly incursions by politicians. The arts coalition in South Carolina, the ABC partnership, was created by three leaders from arts, education and the university, but added a new leader from a university dance program and chose a replacement for the university director (Mitchell, 2000). The association of school councils in Chicago is a threat to the control of the school system exercised by Mayor Daley that is compounded with charges of corruption against the coordinator, Sheila Castillo, a Latino parent, former city of Chicago employee, and active council member (Diana Lauber, personal communication, May, 1997).

The political situation in Chicago means local organizations are in conflict with large political powers. The MacArthur Foundation supplied a grant for the formation of the Chicago Association of Local School Councils. In 1995, a first convention focused on school leadership: "creating nurturing classrooms" and "positive" schools, developing "planning, monitoring and evaluation schedules," and becoming advocates by defining problems, finding the right person to hear these problems, and continuing to motivate supporters (Chicago Association of Local School Councils, n.d.).

Practical advice varies depending on what type of leader and what form of organization is involved. In contrast to the political concerns of groups in Chicago, a neutral adviser stresses the advisability of "pre-meetings" with parents and community leaders so they can learn about professional staff and how they talk (North Central Educational Laboratory, n.d.). A similar rule requires that there be no substitutes for members of the smaller executive committee because middle-level management may be either less committed to partnerships or less able to mobilize resources for them (Mitchell, 1990).

Protest against central decision-makers requires confrontations and court action

(Mitchell, 1996). To bring parents or other activists into school councils is a giant step, but for them to become members of the association of councils means they are further along than most parents and are becoming 'professional volunteers.' Ideological convictions, including religion, as well as pay for part-time jobs, are often a part of the reason for parents becoming council members (Bonito Street, interview, May 12, 1995). For volunteer leaders to take the next leap requires leadership experiences, which organizations controlled by professionals do not provide. For example in Alberta, Canada, a school council manual, produced in limited numbers, is distributed by the Department of Learning, formerly the Department of Education.

In order to become active in the association of councils, parents must have outside support. Where schools are linked to religion, there is a larger structure in which a local partnership can benefit. In an Australian case study, a residential Lutheran school brings students and consultants from great distances while the school organizes a variety of partnerships in the small rural community (Kilpatrick, et al., 2002). The Catholic church provides the possibilities of similar partnerships in many countries.

In order to operate federated councils or partnerships as part of a church organization, training is needed for local board members. Increasingly, such support is provided by foundations or business groups. Training programs for this purpose exist in many places, but few opportunities for actual decision making exist. Charter schools with boards, such as private schools, provide such opportunities (Mitchell, 2001b). The appeal of charter schools to Afro-Americans and, probably, Aboriginal Canadians suggests control of schools may be an important experience in learning to make decisions.

More limited opportunities are provided by Key Communicator programs in public schools, which function similar to an association of councils (Mitchell, 1996). The question is whether a Key Communicator has the right to make decisions, and is an association of school councils a part of school governance? Any federation of councils must provide more than a sense of participating in decisions already made.

THE LEADERS OF MOVEMENTS

A different kind of leader is needed to develop democratic and community associations as federal or secondary-level groupings. Transforming changes seems to suggest the most influential people will be those who work across turfs of either organizations or knowledge (Mitchell, 1995). Organic leaders or transformative intellectuals are suggested by a number of theorists as providing an alternative to experts who claim a scientific basis for working with hierarchical organizations that are separate from the community.

Organic leaders grasp a vision of the way all of the forces in a community act together; they also relate present struggles to past conflicts. Leaders who move back and forth between institutions and foundations and who create new groups, are particularly close to such ideal intellectuals, such as Ann Hallett, former Executive Director of the Cross City Campaign for Urban School Reform. Mrs. Hallett has been an executive with an advocacy organization, a foundation, and a business; she currently lives in Seattle and Chicago and has wide experience in a number of different places. Because of uprooting from past movements, Chicago's intellectuals only occasionally have such ties to their traditions, including religion.

The connection of education to the other institutions is grasped by intellectuals with roots in traditions and with links to the people. Organic leaders who link the past and the future are like the social movements on behalf of which they speak and plan. New leaders act together in order to complement each other. Organic leaders direct and nourish the changes in which they are involved and for which they act as catalysts. The best examples are found in countries, such as Vietnam, where leaders have undergone changes from colonial administrations to communism and towards an independent future. Working through regime changes, several teachers and educators in Vietnam developed multigrade materials and approaches for working with many ethnic groups that were similar to those from which they themselves came (Moyneux & Wooley, 2004).

The needs of ethnic minority children in Vietnam had long been championed by a group of committed teachers and education officials both in Hanoi and in the provinces with sizable ethnic minorities. This commitment was overseen by the Research Centre for Ethnic Minority Education (RCEME). Dr. Trysan Sy Nguyen, the now retired Director of the RCEME, recalls how he moved from being a civil servant in Hanoi to answering the call of President Ho Chi Minh in 1959 to work in mountainous areas with seven ethnic minorities, the main one being Hmong.

Under Dr. Nguyen's leadership, the research centre built up a team including Mr. Pham Vu Kich, a senior staff member who had 14 years' teaching experience in ethnic minority communities, and Ms.Tran Thi Thanh, Dr. Nguyen's key assistant and advisor, who was a highly regarded ethnic minority teacher. These central administrators were joined by provincial officials, such as Mr. Dang who began as a member of the Kinh ethnic group and worked for many other communities for over 40 years. These local and experienced people sought help from international educators from UNICEF, such as the Education Project Officer, Mr. Hoang Van Sit and, eventually, Australian Educators. A visionary leader with UNICEF Vietnam leader is Dr. Elaine Furniss, its Education Project Officer. On her arrival in Hanoi in 1993, she fostered partnerships with key personnel in the Ministry of Education and Training in Vietnam to achieve this. Dr. Furniss sought international models for program improvement through teacher training.

The consultancy team from Australia had three members. Two of these, Keith Pigdon and Marilyn Woolley, were teacher educators with the Faculty of Education at The University of Melbourne. The third member, Paul Molyneux had been teaching in inner city Melbourne primary schools in low socio-economic status communities characterized by their high numbers of students from diverse linguistic and cultural backgrounds. Woolley and Pigdon worked with Furniss on teacher education and materials development projects in Australia. Furniss was familiar with the staged remote area where Woolley and Pigdon conducted Aboriginal teacher education workshops; groups of teachers from Vietnam then visited these areas.

Similar to the Vietnam situation, organic leaders emerge in groups or from partnerships. In North America, Chicago is the strongest example of a broad movement affecting educational reform. It is said that this movement involved many ordinary people, but was carried out by small tightly bound groups similar to the early Christian church. For example, Sokoni Karanja, who led a Peoples' Movement to protest teacher strikes in an early stage of school reform in Chicago and, later, developed a ritual alternative to gangs, defers to his partner, Ben Kendrick, an analyst and critic who runs a series of social agencies (Sokoni Karanja, interview, April 4, 1994). Kendrick is a behind-the-scenes figure in school reform who links to the first editor of *Catalyst*, Linda Lentz, and the organization publishing it.

Other more typical leader groups involve women. Although more like expert facilitators, the three women who planned the Orr project are similar to others who became more political. Two political women who were active in Chicago reform, and who complemented each other, were Joan Slay and Corretta McFerren. In actual lobbying against changes in the Illinois legislation for 1993, Joan Slay was the director who coordinated the lobbying of principals and other organizations like a chess game. Coretta McFerren articulated the feelings of those present and tried to get everyone, including me, involved in the political process. Both were linked to powerful men: Ben Kindrick sponsored Corretta McFerren and Don Moore directed Joan Slay.

Neither woman links directly to the past. Corretta says that Joan was trained by Alinsky, while she learned from Alinsky's students. Joan says very little about herself (C. McFerren, interview, October 26, 1993). Joan has died of cancer; many other women followed her in becoming active in the Chicago reform movement (Aimee Horton, personal communication, November, 2001). When the reformers met to plan their lobbying in 1993, only a handful of men were present.

Men play the symbolic roles in reform while women carry on the battles. Men who initiate reform and who die in the process, such as those in Chicago or Kentucky, become martyrs for reform; a fate denied to women (L. Lens, interview, October 5, 1993). The women in the community organizations inspire each other and the men involved in the cause (Mitchell, 1996). Men and women provide different forms of organic leadership in the mysterious mix of change and partnerships.

Neither leaders nor followers are alone because they work together in social movements. Organic leaders for education create alternatives to accepted ways of thinking. One of the accepted ways of developing support for the education is co-opting businesspeople around campaigns to mobilize communities for broader purposes (Mitchell, 2000a; Larson, 1997). When teachers, other professionals, and community members sense that the time is right for action, they will become masters of their own destiny and change education. Groups of active women try to become organic leaders by drawing parallels to changes in society that might promote support for arts education. Jane Alexander, as Chairperson of the National Endowment for the Arts, suggested that there is a need in the arts to create a parallel campaign to the "green revolution" designed by environmentalists to protect the natural world (Larson, 1997, p. 143). A radical alternative for arts education requires changes as sweeping as environmentalists want for the planet.

Social movements in the arts develop with an awareness of both discontent and possibilities for improvement. An individual stage of "being divided no more" leads to individuals discovering one another in small groups, such as discussed among women in Chicago reform (Palmer, 1998, p. 166). Those seeking a sense of community need to find or be offered a vision. The group sessions, which in most movements precede public positions, are difficult to organize. A general awareness of cultural needs occurs as a result of mass meetings or public involvement on television. Links between art and the environment, such as plays about pollution, support group cohesion in communities in the swamp between Georgia and Florida (Mitchell, 2000a).

Although the role of women is obvious in arts education, the focus for single movements in particular places is not as clear. Celebrations of achievement in the arts or education show the common position, values, and alternative rewards that are emerging (Mitchell, 2000a). The development of a common cause occurs through interaction and new symbols, rather than debate and traditional beliefs. Arts education would have to draw more on the artists in street entertainment to find its creative will. The leaders of general social movements perceive new relationships between people, resources, and nature. Past traditions may be reworked to overcome tensions and develop new codes. The Coalition of Essential Schools is, in this sense, a revitalization movement as much as economic and social changes in underdeveloped countries (Moncey & McQuillan, 1990). Divisions among educators as well as isolation from other social movements is a limitation on education becoming a movement for change (Mitchell, 2000).

STUDENTS AS EXPRESSIVE LEADERS

Social movements may focus on expression as much as on action. For students, social movements overcome their isolation and alienation if the expression of students is important for their education and if their ideas are valued by the adult leaders who act on behalf of students. The language of students is personal and expressive, rather than abstract and instrumental (Mitchell, 1990). It is the relationship and style that is primary for adolescents.

Student leaders begin by expressing their experiences rather than leading adults. Creating video films is a current interest of students in rural and urban areas where they try to develop their interpretations of their own experiences (Mitchell, 2002b). Many students see their experience in high school as like being in prison; the arts change prisons and are able to change schools. Visual symbols, drama, and expressive music may overcome this alienation. In Chicago, for example, the student publication *New Expression* features the arts and contests in the arts (Mitchell, 1996).

Student interests may be tapped to transform the appearance of schools, a concern for many students (Mitchell, 1990). In a Chicago attempt to integrate public housing, education, and city parks, elementary students worked with landscape architects to create a new playground plan that would transform one of the worst schools and areas of Chicago (Greg Darnieder, interview, October 17, 1993). Their outdoor learning centre would include tennis and basketball courts, an outdoor theatre, a community garden, and a "walk of fame."

Improving schools should focus on supporting students, preventing their alienation, and drawing lessons from the past. Every student would benefit from a "happening" as was experienced by students at the historic Black Mountain College in North Carolina between the two World Wars (Harris, 1987, p. 259). Creative expression should be combined with efforts to enrich old buildings, such as dramas, murals or brightly painted walls. The buildings would then become the setting for discussion, controversy and personal realization, which is the core of social movements.

In Chicago, gang members are involved in school elections by demonstrating as 21st Century Votes and running candidates for school council (Mitchell, 1996). A few were elected as council members, but most gang members were rejected. A social activist used this experience to develop an alternative to gangs. Sokoni Karanja, says: "The real problem is that the gangs have a product, and we don't: They are selling safety, camaraderie, employment, a group that shares a set of values—all the things that teenagers look for" (Weissman, 1993, November, p.6). Karanja organized a program, including the arts, for a puberty-like transition that provides support for the self-image of Afro-American males. His center offers pre-employment counseling, school tutoring, parent counseling, recreational activities, and community development, but a further revitalization was needed to match the appeal of gangs.

Students need the support of partnerships; they also respond to the ritual and recognition that religion traditionally offers. Students' involvement in movements is unpredictable because they are marginal to the partnership efforts. Unlike life in gangs, the world of foundations, multiple partnerships, and international efforts is distant from them. Specific partnerships provide an opportunity for them to link with these more complex partners. Students must be included if the broader partnerships are to succeed. Federal systems of partnerships and adult advocacy groups are the 'glass ceiling' for student activists. This limitation can be overcome since it is similar to student representation on state boards of education, discussed in Chapter 3.

Chapter 5
Inspirations

I am always being told to suggest something feasible. What in effect is being said to me is that I should propound the ordinary methods or at least combine something good with the existing evil – Jean Jacques Rousseau (Boyd, 1956, p.6)

Partnerships provide an opportunity for educators to get beyond their usual ways of thinking. People who are caught in the procedures may not seize these opportunities. Those on the margins of schools are better able to see the possibilities of change. Questions about why or what happens if we do the opposite of current policies increase the options for future actions. For example, in the Accelerated School Project, enrichment is provided for struggling students (Mitchell, 1998); this approach contrasts with the typical practice of giving low achievers work sheets that deprives them of opportunities for richer learning.

Other examples of unexpected approaches include curriculum leaders being evaluated by teachers in order to improve the teachers' own methods. A different philosophy leads to a different view of schools. The values of a place, including beauty, environment, and history, reveal the unique advantages of a rural school for education (Mitchell, 2000b). The imagery, sociability, and bright clothes of adolescents in slums may be a basis for hope to teachers as it is for these students (Mitchell, 1990). Constructive criticism, alternatives, and deficiencies may each provide opportunities for educators to develop fresh perspectives.

Appreciation of outstanding people may become a basis for change. Outstanding teachers are supported by renewal centers. Teacher networks promise to stop the loss of their innovations with their retirement or death. The concrete experiences of teachers could be the basis from which experts develop their plans, rather than expecting teachers to follow their abstract models. Teachers may connect with larger organizations or groups in the society in order to challenge discrimination within schools.

Female teachers and reformers promote partnership movements, but women may experience discrimination within partnerships. Although the inclusion of girls and the recognition of women is a world-wide concern, innovations and partnerships continue to neglect the interests of women. Most reform projects rely on women, and the integration of the innovations into social movements often occurs as a result of the efforts by women in small groups. Women inside existing partnerships are often not aware of the extent to which their concerns are unappreciated.

The future of partnerships depends upon seeing similar limits and moving beyond them. Those inside partnerships can see themselves as outsiders do and outsiders must think in terms of the internal view of partners. Criticism and suggestions from the outside may then be more meaningful. Ironically, students may be appreciated as they study outstanding adults as models for the future rather than in terms of their own immediate lives. Women could be models in future partnerships that express their different gender ideas. If the status order in education is reversed, new possibilities for learning will be considered. It is also possible to recognize subordinate groups by linking them to others internationally, since they may not be accepted at home.

IMAGE OF THE FUTURE

Thinking about the future occurs when people are no longer in the same situations performing familiar tasks with others they know well. Community projects that include the town hall meetings stressed by the Kettering Foundation allow for a depth discussion that no survey matches (Yankelovich, 1991). Such diverse discussions have been the basis for developing leadership programs.

The first leadership program began in Philadelphia in 1959 (Leadership Ottawa, 2002a). There are now over 1,000 leadership programs worldwide, indicating how easily these programs spread (Susan Sparks, interview, August 19, 2002). Those outside of North America are primarily located in Commonwealth countries and the

European Common Market. They are similar to the National Writing Program discussed in Chapter 4. Community meetings focus on the universal need to develop future leaders (Community Leadership Association, n.d.).

In Canada, the J. W. McConnell Family Foundation (2002) supports the development of new community networks as a basis for communities planning for the future. Attempting to develop a sense of trusteeship for the future, Vancouver started the first program in 1991 and Calgary followed in 1998. In 1999 and 2000, the McConnell Foundation supported programs in ten Canadian communities. By 2002, 14 Canadian cities had this program operating.

The Canadian coordinators meet annually as does the international organization. The coordinators talk frequently and, as a result, often develop close relationships (Susan Sparks, interview, August 19, 2002). The Calgary coordinator has worked with a number of non-profit organizations, and has a liberal arts degree in history and English. She believes the women working with other community leadership programs benefit from having more than a single organization as a base.

These community leadership programs are based on a transforming view of leadership. Present problems with the environment or politics are discussed in order to find a larger framework to which such problems can be related. Issues crossing sectors and organizations, such as poverty, require new coalitions (Leadership Calgary, 2002a). Leadership for the community's future is believed to require different settings and a cross-section of participants. Leadership Calgary brings educational leaders together with those from social agencies, the United Way, and non-profit organizations, such as AIDS Awareness Association, and businesses, including the Calgary Herald newspaper (Samuel Mitchell, presentation for Leadership Calgary, December 7, 2000).

One participant, Brian Huskins, says, "It is about changing the way we think: creating environments for learning in the classroom, in the family, and in the community...finding a way to have each of these components of learning complement each other...." (Huskins, 1999). An 18 year old student, Chris Healy created a fellowship of skateboarders, his interest at the time, but he went on to volunteer for many city services, such as the Winter Festival. Other young leaders are establishing non-profit centers, counseling other students, creating web sites, and becoming politically active in their community (Leadership Calgary, 2002a).

Chris and other young people in the program are supported to "create social capital" as a Generation V intern by a federal Canadian government program to engage in the voluntary sector (Ibid). Bursary support for people who participate comes from the Junior League, local foundations, companies, the United Way, and private individuals. Other sponsors for the entire program include the Chamber of Commerce, the Royal Bank, and prominent oil companies.

Although the sponsors emphasize the volunteer role, participants in Leadership Calgary are not controlled by volunteer coordinators or professionals. The participants work together, draw on their extensive networks, and plan their own programs and presentations in monthly programs (Dale Erickson, personal communication, July 17, 2002). They have a "wonderful experience" in becoming leaders who continue to communicate with other participants after the program and, as alumni, are welcomed into the current activities.

Alumni are seen as disruptive by traditional organizations, including the Calgary Board of Education. The coordinator of the program, Suzie Sparks, finds the challenge that alumni bring to traditional organizations surprising (Interview, August 19, 2002). The organization does train its participants in the politics of change and how to mobilize support for new policies.

APPRECIATIVE INQUIRY

Unlike the leadership programs, Image Chicago arranges its projects with separate community and school groups. The founder, Bliss Browne, engages teachers, parents, community members, and planners in retreats and meetings. Like other innovators, Browne underwent a series of conversion experiences. She gave up divinity school to work in social service, and chucked parish work to become a banker. She was Division Head of the First National Bank of Chicago, when her "insides turned around" (Belsie, 2001). She found appreciation theory after a retreat experience with Bread for the World and a severance package from the bank for nine months. In 1992, the new baby of Imagine Chicago was born when Mrs. Browne brought 20 educators, corporate executives, community organizers, and volunteers together.

An academic, David Cooperrider, strongly influenced the choice of appreciation theory (Cooperrider & Whitney, n.d.). After talking to the survivors of Hiroshima in Japan, Cooperrider looked for a goal in organizational theory that could be as positive as the bomb was negative. He saw that other organizational theories, including action research, are based on "problems." Other social action approaches in Chicago, including the followers of Saul Alinsky, derive from a view of people as having "deficits," such as lacking power.

In order to bind those with power and status together with those who lack it, appreciation theory has exceptional people scrutinized by those who seek success. Appreciation uses the best experiences of the most successful members as understood by the least experienced and lowest status group to formulate what the finest future might be. The two groups must communicate or "construct" a new world.

A focus on schools has brought many of these groups together. Schools and museums cooperate to improve the reading comprehension of students and develop communities through imaginative leaps by parents and volunteers (Ihejirika, 2000). Partnerships with museum are similarly emphasized by Howard Gardner in his development of alternatives to schools. In Imagine Chicago, parents come to shape the city, rather than being an object for planners. They come to think of themselves as "creators of the cities future" (Appreciative Inquiry Commons, 1999). 50 students from over half of Chicago's poorer neighborhoods interviewed 140 outstanding artists, media executives, civic, business, political, and business leaders, and other young people. The leaders are the "glue" for the community's future.

The program of Imagine Chicago follows appreciation theory in order to learn from successes how to develop in the future. Organizations are the "catalysts" to enhance this process (Ibid). In 1995, as a result of a grant from the Annenberg foundation, Imagine Chicago began working with schools. Science museums are for them the means to provoke innovation within the educational system. Communication between participants is the aim, rather than driving students reading scores higher. Students and teachers become involved with nature, not just themselves. By working with museums, appreciation theory constructed a new understanding of people as a part of nature.

Imagine Chicago creates schools that integrates the sciences with the curriculum as much as artists linked with lessons (Ihejirika, 2000). A kindergarten teacher, Jana Baskins, says her students can learn their colors from worksheets or go to the nature centre to see variations among flowers. Using a digital camera, young people use pictures to tell their stories to the teacher who writes them, while they also learn counting and record keeping from their own experiences. Following this program, the league of schools looks like museums, since they have so many exhibits. There are five elementary schools, two high schools, and six museums in the league. According to studies by Annenburg and DePaul University, students involved in the program improve in both an Illinois standardized test and the Iowa Tests of Basic Skills.

DePaul University's Center for Urban Education is an important partner for Imagine Chicago; the director helped write the foundation proposal to support Imagine Chicago. (Ibid). DePaul was one of the primary partners for the Orr Project described in Chapter 4. Under the leadership of Barbara Radner, DePaul created teacher networks with poor communities for twenty years (Mitchell, 1998). The program director of Imagine Chicago, Edith Njuguna, came to work with Bliss Browne after four years with the DePaul network. She is a graduate in linguistics and literature of Nairobi University in Kenya and holds a graduate degree from DePaul with a diploma in Hispanic studies from Madrid, Spain.

Although the initial followers of Imagine Chicago came from similar cultures, Ms. Njuguna's background should help her with the different cultural groups in Chicago and around the world. In Birmingham, England, the Human City Institute offers a similar program to Chicago's sister city (Human City Institute, 2001). In September, 2002, the ten years of success by Imagine Chicago were celebrated in Birmingham, Bradford and Swinton in England. Similar projects exist in Los Angeles, Dallas, Washington, and Oakland (Imagine Chicago, 2001).

People follow its web cite (www.imaginechicago.org) as a source for developing projects in other cities and countries on five continents, including Australia, England, Scotland, Denmark, and Yugoslavia (Ibid). A UNICEF project in a remote part of northeast India, Nagaland, led to 7000 community interviews between different generations and a renewed vision and community aim. Business projects develop with programs of interviewing and restructuring on many sites including Avon in Mexico.

Personal accounts of change among people abound. One parent describes herself as a "free person" since she began expressing herself in front of educators (Imagine Chicago, 2001). Parents who become community activists tell similar stories. Mary Burns began a program of field trips for students, Kingas Kamp. She attended the Citizen Leadership program of Imagine Chicago. The future became a program of performing arts for kids, the Miracle Center.

RENEWAL CENTERS FOR TEACHERS

Although community projects recognize teachers and celebrate their success, they also seek support from powerful sponsors. Finding a new way to recognize teachers was the aim of a single teacher, Jean Powell, who was selected to be Teacher-of-the-Year in North Carolina in 1984 (Mitchell, 2000a). She wanted other teachers to be recognized and renewed, which teacher awards fail to do. Teachers selected for the usual teacher rewards are resented by their colleagues (Mitchell, 1998). Teacher awards often mean the recipients leave teaching because of the contacts they make when speaking about peak experiences in teaching.

Jean Powell sought a grant from the state legislature for a centre where teachers would be treated with respect and encouraged to be creative while staying in teaching. Teachers so selected are served their meals on china, and provided a liberal arts program at no cost. The program is modeled after the liberal arts focus of the Aspen Institute in Colorado. The North Carolina Humanities Committee provided support for the request for government assistance as did arts organizations.

When the program was approved and opened in 1986., the North Carolina Center for the Advancement of Teaching (NCCAT) provided teachers with opportunities to be creative in art, myth, dance, and architecture. NCCAT is situated on 30 acres of the Smoky Mountains in the small town of Cullowhee, North Carolina, adjoining Western Carolina University. Its main campus includes a large conference centre, two residence halls, an amphitheater, exercise room, and recreational facilities.

This program offers a humane environment, designed to invigorate teachers. NCCAT offers teachers a collection of paintings and sculpture, a small reading room, and a separate music room. One seminar, "The Design of Earthly Gardens," involves comparing the Nineteenth Century gardens in nearby Asheville with current landscapes. The teachers discuss the arts as equals with experts, such as a landscape architects.

At NCCAT teachers describe the six-day seminar as a peak experience in their lives (Jerry Franson, interview, January 7, 1998). Unlike experts formulating innovations, planners of NCCAT saw the creative potential of teachers, rather than their deficiencies. The director of the center, Mary Jo Utley, stresses that they want teachers to see the world as it might be, rather than as it is. Teacher-students form study circles among themselves to discuss ideas. One alumnus expresses the experience of others after the seminar stating that one is "ready to reenter the long line" (Rud & Oldendorf, 1992, p. 109). Another teacher refers to the centre is a means to reach a personal "center" (Ibid, p. 57).

The NCCAT program reflects current trends in education and demands to service the state. In the 1990s, the curriculum began to include the environment and technology (Preparing North Carolina for 21st Century Schools: Programs, 2000). The environmental activities were related to culture and art. In 1993, a North Carolina Teacher Academy was added that emphasizes leadership, technology, and classroom teaching. NCCAT added an additional center in the Piedmont area in the Northern part of the state and planned a center along the Atlantic coast.

By 2000, NCCAT formed partnerships with other programs within the state as well as beyond. In North Carolina, NCCAT works with the University of North Carolina Center for Leadership Development, the Mathematics and Science Education Network, and the North Carolina Restructuring Initiative in Special Education. With the support of major foundations, such as Ford, and other companies, including BellSouth, NCCAT cooperates with the surrounding states to improve teacher training (Southeast Center for Teaching Quality, 2002).

Nationally and internationally, NCCAT allies itself with the Kenan Best Practices Center which collects research, creates a data base, and shares this information. In turn, the Kenan Center joins with the International Center for Leadership in Education to identify model schools, programs, and policies in the U. S., Europe, and Asia (Kenan Best Practices, n.d.). NCCAT increases its budget through private funding in order to carry out its international programs (Jerry Franson, phone interview, September 17, 1998).

International programs and state-wide partnerships were not considered when Jean Powell began with a dream in 1984 (Mitchell, 2001a). Political advisers told her the project would never be realized. The sixty-five year old teacher won support from three powerful forces to secure a budget request: a governor who was interested in education, the resourceful speaker of the House, and the respected president of the University of North Carolina. In spite of this support, Jean Powell was told the initial request would be reduced or the idea eliminated from the legislative package. In 1985, The governor's request for an initial grant of $2.5 million was passed without any reduction.

In subsequent years, even a restricted economy did not lead to a reduction in the government's support. Controversy exists about NCCAT future expansion at two other additional sites. Rather than NCCAT, should not one of the many educational organizations be asked to develop new sites? The director, May Jo Utley, argues that the partnerships were needed to utilize the original center and would be used in the expansions for the same reason (21st Century Schools, 2002). The North Carolina legislature continues to support NCCAT as a means of retaining quality teachers in the state. A series of similar centers opened in other states, including a new center built on Tampa Bay in St. Petersburg (Jerry Franson, interview, January 7, 1998). Funds for such a center could be raised in Calgary as I suggested to the Dean of Education.

The alumni of the program travel abroad with programs for themselves. They seek corporate support for seminars in other parts of the world, including Canada, England, Mexico, and Costa Rica. After a travel program, several groups of alumni have joined a seminar (Jerry Franson, phone interview, September 17, 1998). The alumni, who together with school superintendents nominate new participants in the North Carolina center, would benefit from linking with another group of teachers in another part of the world in order to share their experiences. Finding support for teacher groups in the South could challenge foundations, businesses, and governments, but it would make teaching excellence a rewarding experience in the poorest country.

NETWORKS OF TEACHERS

Similar to NCCAT, other teacher networks bring teachers and administrators together through informal meetings and technological connections. Direct teacher contacts would require a greater number of teachers than would be involved in going through the Byzantine world of educational organizations. For example, IMPACT II, founded in 1979, has become a teacher network that reaches a half million teachers through 25 sites (Education Week, 1999). Two women teachers play a dominant role in IMPACT II: Ellen Myers and Ellen Dempsey.

Like NCCAT, female teachers play key roles in forming these networks. Neither gender nor any other related issue is a political focus of teacher network programs. The new networks worry about calling themselves 'progressive educators' since this label might turn some people away (Mitchell, 1998). Unlike the humanistic emphasis of teacher renewal centers, in IMPACT II there is a prevalence of shop talk about the profession.

Similar to informal networkers examined on the internet, IMPACT II is concerned with teaching required schools subjects. It is the "recipes" that teachers can exchange that are at the heart of the approach (Meyers & McIssac, 1994, pp. 15, 79). A "Blue Plate Special" of ideas for the classroom is advertised. The exchanges between teachers reflect progressive education ideas, such as a student citizenship project or schools within schools. Through conferences or electronic bulletin boards, IMPACT II seeks new ways to communicate with teachers.

Impact II is a bridge between the world of the experts and the workplace of teachers. Reports are drawn from new journals and recent studies. The work of Howard Gardner on multiple intelligence or the ideas of Linda Darling-Hammond on teacher leaders is typical. Teachers who are also writers, such as Nancy Atwell, are important because they are models for encouraging other teachers to write.

Teachers accept a division among themselves between initiators and adapters of change that echo expert and teacher social distances. It is a mentor relationship among teachers that is most frequently demonstrated in their materials. IMPACT II makes small grants both to mentor teachers who develop and write about their ideas and to other teachers who adopt them. The innovators receive grants worth fifty percent more than the grants given to the adopters (Bradley, 1989). Although only a few hundred dollars are involved, teachers continue to separate innovation from adoption.

The network teachers follow the methods and assumptions of male experts. The pilot programs were assessed by Dale Mann at Columbia University (Bradley, 1989). In 1987, a four-year study by the National Diffusion Network led to recognition of Impact II as an effective approach for professional development. The evaluations and continuing search for professional "indicators" show an abstract professional concern. IMPACT II draws on traditional logical thinking rather than multiple intelligence stressed in its discussion of theories, whether it is the handbooks for teachers, videos, or the interactive television program of the menu on the internet [http://www.teachnet.org].

NCCAT conferences are designed for idea-centred teachers, who may, for example, be interested in cyberspace. A concern for professional ideas promoted by IMPACT II has not led to policy changes. The Teachers Voice Initiative was inspected to provide a "teacher's voice to the national dialogue on school reform" (Meyers & McIssac, 1994, p. 4). Neither this program nor any similar ones have been implemented. The Institute for the Future of Education attracted 50 teachers from across the country and positively affected those attending. However, there was no vision that might

to teachers of at-risk students.

The editors of the Impact II study speak of surveys which show that most teachers feel they are "targets" of educational reform (Ibid, p. 5). Teachers often want to reduce the number of innovations, including partnerships, in which they are expected to be involved. Teacher action against those who make teachers targets or victims is not stressed by IMPACT II. Nor is there more than incidental contact with other teacher groups across the world.

In terms of professional literature and action based on it, educational research shows teachers to be deficient (Mitchell, 1998). Exceptional teachers who could be appreciated for the future should be a focus for new research. The future would then be more than a repetition of the present. The lessons from Volunteer Calgary and Imagine Chicago could be a pattern whereby the best teachers are studied to prepare scenarios for the future.

THE ACCELERATED SCHOOL PROJECT

Concern for correcting the inequalities in education and creating new possibilities for educators working together are features of the Accelerated Schools Project which shows itself open to a wide range of ideas and groups. In 1986, the radical economist, Henry Levin, developed the program as a way of reversing the usual approach whereby the poorer students are given repetitive and structured material, while gifted students are provided enriched and varied assignments (Northwest Regional Education Laboratory, 2001). Levin cooperates with other advocates, something that is exceptional among promoters who seem to fear rivals. Among organizations with a plan for change, this project is exceptional in obtaining Ford Foundation support for an independent evaluation by the Manpower Demonstration Research Corporation.

Such diverse thinking means that, at most, 700 of the 1300 schools following the Accelerated Process are similar (Viadero, 2002). In treating at-risk students as exceptional, the program stresses purposes or visions for empowerment, often through school-based management; and builds upon the strengths of students, parents, and communities, rather than focusing on their deficiencies. In order to initiate the program in a school, eighty percent or more of the teachers must support the program. Later, the school council required consensus on decisions and the involvement of teachers through task forces for new initiatives. Because of concern for school government and parent participation, an evaluation study of seven schools found that student achievement differences did not occur until after two years were spent developing these program supports (Viadero, 2002).

Are government and participation supports essential in a democratic society? Are standardized test results more important than democracy? A program that targets high poverty families, ESL students, and special education needs is most successful with middle-ability students (Bloom, et al., 2001). A program that is based on the needs of at-risk students who are a problem because they become unemployed, experience poverty, drop out of school, receive public assistance, become unwed parents, and are more often arrested does not measure progress to overcoming any of these problems (Hopfenberg, et al., 1993).

SOCIAL INDICATORS

While the young people are in school, arrests or school discipline problems can be measured. Considering that only five years were used in measuring school results, some follow-up of at-risk students after leaving school would be reasonable. Levin could follow European partnerships and use social indicators for his results (The European Commission Education, 1999).

In Levin's theory, empowerment is a crucial part of his vision; his schools attempt to enhance the perception of strengths among those living in poverty. There are no studies of personal power in partnerships, although perceptions by people of themselves are important in the European work. Self-conceptions of the poor and their participation in the community need to be further researched in both continents (European Commission Education, 1999).

How the disadvantaged perceive opportunities depends on how they see themselves (Mitchell, 1990). This question can be related to social studies. When civics is considered, community participation becomes a part of the academic course. Non-governmental organizations see community programs as involving more than academic tasks; they are a basis for rebuilding the community. For Levin's project, the school is influenced by the community, but is not measured by its contribution to it.

The relationship between the change agents and their subjects was not considered as a research topic. Measures of change, social indicators, depend on the values and ideology of the educators and researchers (Cobb & Rixford, 1998). The discussion of George Washington University students showed that change agents and poor communities need to develop reciprocal relationships. The involvement of the school in community associations should equal the volunteers'contribution to the school. Students would benefit from both types of exchanges.

The program for schools includes involvement, creativity, and reciprocal ties. Accelerated schools combine traditional emphasis on ceremonies with a modern stress on individual reflection. A variety of reflections aims to prevent simple copying among schools or between students. Celebrations and parades are organized to mark the creation of a new Accelerated School site. In one site, teachers dressed up in historical costumes borrowed from a local theatre group (Mitchell, 1998).

Attempts to honour individuals, such as a particular volunteer, combine festival and individual approaches (Mitchell, 2000a). Teachers are encouraged to recognize the worth of individuals in the community so that those in the community will, in turn, help them in their individual classrooms and school projects. Afternoon sessions are, on occasion, turned over to community members and university volunteers for teaching special topics while teachers meet and plan. The transformation of a schoolyard becomes a visual symbol of the changed relationship between the school and its community.

Involvement in the school culture is an important index of change in these schools. The renewal of a commitment initiates new members of the school community, incorporating art as an essential part of the process (Ibid). The use of ritual is typical of religious partnerships, but no religious organization is involved with Levin's project. In a variety of settings, students are given opportunities to share the project's vision. An accelerated school pledge is followed by a special song that a music teacher wrote. In another setting, students make collages and drawings, contribute a hand to a giving tree to which every student attaches a hand, place Accelerated symbols on t-shirts, folders or mugs, or dress up and act out parts of the vision as "guiding hands, touching hearts, and unlocking minds" (Accelerated School Project, 1993, p. 16).

The students' visions become more varied as the program spreads into middle schools (Ibid). For example, after everyone develops student cards to display on the wall, students present a "creations:" songs, essays, poems, crests and raps. The students show both independence and creativity while participating in the Accelerated School Project. Creations embody the vision of the school for students; they help them overcome the pervasive pessimism regarding the abilities of students from poor families. This variety can be measured and appears to be an important part of the program's evolution.

This and related programs can be guided by a realistic evaluation of what is required to change the lot of the poor. Poverty results from compounding of failures through three generations (Mitchell, 1995). The British have a saying that to move out of the working class it takes three generations to acquire the skills, the language, and sense of personal competence. Although social mobility may be more rapid in North America, the project could establish the possibility for empowerment of each generation: grandparents, parents, and students. Each group could take steps that include personal empowerment, mutual cooperation, and heightened aspirations for themselves and their community.

External and personal measures are available to guide these transitions (Cobb & Rixford, 1998). For example in environmental studies, community members are acting solely as reporters (Joyce & Calhoun, 1996). In the Accelerated School Project, they are equally capable of measuring specific changes in their communities, but it is the teachers who do the research and go into the community (Mitchell, 1998). When the teachers do a survey, the students do learn from their example about how to do research, including the use of control groups.

The teachers are in control. They teach parents to be effective volunteers, as well as college students and businesspeople who become "Friday Faculty." The whole school is capable of involving the community, including older students who help younger ones in their studies. Power needs to be given to the parents, students, and community members; staff will be surprised to see what they can contribute to teachers' professional development.

As discussed in Chapter 3, throughout the United States, community members are becoming contributors to teachers in-service programs. When teachers become a part of community development, they broaden their thinking so that they speak about themselves as members of the community. Community development and broader cooperation could, as well, teach Henry Levin to see people in poverty as such people see themselves.

Dr. Levin supports a number of projects, other than his own. He is an enthusiastic supporter of Different Ways of Knowing, a program based on Gardner's ideas of multiple intelligence offered by the Galef Institute (Mitchell, 1998). Levin has a similar school that develops the arts. This school offers a music conservatory in the afternoons and on Saturdays mostly for at-risk students.

The cooperation between the Accelerated Schools and the Galef project was expected to be a forerunner for some exciting cross-fertilization of ideas among reform groups. A group of five partners were to receive five-year funding from the Annenberg foundation (Mitchell, 2000a). The partners included arts alliances in Chicago, North Carolina, and Nashville. The cancellation of the grant by Annenberg polarized the prospective partners.

Galef's original partner, The Accelerated Schools Project, salvaged an important project in Kentucky (Nancy Huffstutter, e-mail, August 5, 1998). As a result of that cooperation, Governor Paul Patton of Kentucky named a high-risk school, the Engelhard Elementary School, as the recipient of the Education Award in the Arts (The Collaborative, 2001). This collaboration is productive because the former Galef unit, the Collaborative for Teaching and Learning, is now independent of the founding organization.

Aside from cooperation with Galef, Levin and his associates are increasing the number of partners with whom they work. Levin cooperates with one project incorporating technology and another effort to coordinate all major reform partnerships, including the Coalition of Essential Schools (Intel Corporation, 2002; Mitchell, 1998). The ideas of the Accelerated School Project are spreading to other groups working with at-risk students, such as in Edmonton, Canada. However, this project has no international affiliates. The possible retirement of Dr. Levin further limits its possible expansion.

AN INTERNAL PRESSURE GROUP

Neither broader thinking nor commitment to a reform project will in itself change a system which is resistant to change. Future action for change builds on current decisions. Organized pressure brings about change in schools from either inside or outside by community groups. Change from within schools by advocates is unusual.

Internal groups could organize on various equity issues, including gender. Such a pressure group effects cooperation with the administrative hierarchy. Higher administrators offer many rewards, which is a powerful incentive for conformity (Mitchell, 1998). Administrators usually protect themselves from outsiders by a variety of devices: preparing policy reports before considering specific complaints, delaying action on complaints until their own alternative solution is ready to be put into place, arranging material to arrive at a "stacked deck solution" or pretending to make a decision when the outcome is predetermined (McGivney & Haught, 1972).

The Calgary Board of Education used similar tactics to avoid dealing with complaints about gender bias (Steele & Boyle, 1997). Between 1973 and 1989, the question of promotion of female teachers into administration was discussed and dismissed. A series of reports showed discrimination against women. The report in 1989 showed no change in the position of women. A senior administrator proposed an Inquiry on Opportunities for Women, which would monitor the problem for another five years! This proposal would use research to avoid action.

After conducting a survey, publishing statistics on administrative positions by gender, and inviting in an expert to give her views, the Inquiry realized that no progress was being made (Ibid). In 1992, it recommended that a Special Advisor on Women's Issues be appointed and that, in the future, all superintendents prepare reports on their accomplishments of the past year and plans for the future year. The Special Advisor was responsible to the Chief Superintendent and a continuing Gender Equity Committee. The Committee replaced the Inquiry and represented all employee groups.

The new plan was to ensure that an inequity would not be a continuing consideration. The broad representation widened the constituency that would seek corrective action. This representation led to other issues besides advancement being discussed. Gay rights, support staff, male teachers in elementary schools, and sexual attacks were issues that were brought out. The title of the Special Advisor was changed to reflect the concern for all gender issues. The advisor raised issues that people had not previously been discussing, such as the prejudice against women by female administrators who act like males.

The broad representation and wide-ranging issues led to the Special Advisor becoming an "ombudsperson" for people's concerns (Ibid). Gender discrimination was linked to prejudice against immigrants, gays and lesbians, the disabled and racial minorities. Continuing contacts are made with all of these groups, including students and classroom teachers. The conference, *Enabling Visions*, brought out the concerns and anxieties of junior high girls together with the concerns of female teachers being considered for promotion. Surprisingly, students saw a common gender interest with their teachers and their advancement.

On the original issue of promotion, progress was made by Special Advisors working with the Committee. The individuals chosen to be Special Advisors contributed to opening up the forum. The Special Advisors used stories, analogies and metaphors, and their own commitment to convey the message of gender equity. By 1997, the percentage of women in leadership positions was approaching their proportional numbers in teaching (Ibid). The procedures for promotion were monitored by the Committee.

The Committee and the Calgary Board of Education were watched and evaluated by the Conservative government that opposed any extension of gay rights (Mitchell, 1998). In 1998, opposition to the program mounted when stories about gay teens appeared in the local newspaper (U. Steele, email, August 8, 2002). The position of Special Advisor was eliminated for budgetary considerations; bureaucracy reestablished control by using an approach that does not deal with reasons, only money (Sharon Kimmel, personal communication, August 8, 2002).

Public support for the gender program was never created. Neither the Liberal opposition nor the press were aware of the program and were not mobilized to defend it (Mitchell, 1998). The program represented those within the system who wanted their voices heard and actions taken, but it could not continue without allies in the community. Partnerships and voluntary organizations that work outside the system are often more successful in building their constituents into a lobby.

Worldwide concern about discrimination against females is frequently carried out by non-governmental agencies acting with professional and governmental organizations. Save The Children states that "girls education is not just a matter of concern for educations - it is everybody's business"" (2002). Other programs provide scholarships and supports for girls, but involve the construction of an infrastructure, such as roads, that makes possible the continuation of the education of women who are isolated (United States Agency for International Development, 1999). Other programs involve the matching of employers with schools. Everywhere, the role of voluntary organizations acting for girls is accentuated, including teacher training.

In less developed countries, non-governmental organizations range from the local to the colossal in underdeveloped countries (Oxfam, n.d.). The National Literacy Movement in India mobilizes 10 million volunteers, but is largely limited to the southern states of India. It has modest success in increasing literacy. Other approaches have higher success with smaller populations. The removal of a professional qualification requirement and the substitution of community control are evident in Egypt. In rural communities where the enrollment rates are as low as 15 percent among girls, community schools increase enrollment in excess of 70 percent. In the same program, four pilot schools achieve a 100 per cent success rate for passing exams from grade one, compared to 33 percent in government schools. Similarly in Pakistan, community schools are thought to be better by parents because they teach in English and offer science education (Rizvi & Sayee, 2004). Although schools with NGO support are intended for girls, parents want superior education more for boys.

Programs assisted by NGOs increased the self-esteem of girls, their enrollment, and exam results (United States Agency for International Development, 1999). The same programs involve parents and often help them to become literate. Women in communities decide the issues and work with new professional women who expect to work with parents and community activists. Although the variety of local standards is to be expected, issues for women in urban and rural communities are evaluated to overcome their long-term subordination, including building the infrastructure that allows them to travel and participate in formal or informal education.

Ironically, gender is seldom considered a direct issue for the educational reformers in North America. In Chicago, the parent Civic Committee under Lawrence Howe took control of the Leadership for Quality Education (LQE). President Diana Nelson responded to this action and resigned in protest. LQE was charged with being too community orientated and too critical of the school system's budget (Diana Lauber, April 8, 1994). In this case, the issue of gender was not raised. Among the six women who worked at LQE, there was clear discrimination; all of the staff were denied severance pay if they rejected alternative positions with the Civic Committee (Diana Lauber, interview, November 23, 1993). Two white men, Howe and John Ayers, were making the decisions about the futures of six white women on staff and one black woman assistant (Mitchell, 1996). It was believed that charges of gender bias would further divide the movement for reform.

As Chapter 4 shows, the Chicago reform movement is composed of women who work in pairs and triads. In lobbying against changes in the Illinois legislation of 1993, Joan Slay was the director who coordinated the lobbying like a chess game, while Coretta McFerren articulated supporters' feelings and kept them involved 'in the game,' as it were. Both women are influenced by male experts to whom they were responsible (Coretta McFerren, interview, October 26, 1993). The subsequent lack of financial support for Joan Slay when she was dying of cancer by the male executive, Don Moore, raises further questions about male dominance in partnerships (Aimee Horton, personal communication, November, 2001).

Reforms in other situations are carried out by a very large number of women who run the related business, civic, community, and educational organizations. Dedicated women are critical in many program areas, particularly art education (Mitchell, 2000a). However, these reform efforts are so widely separated from earlier feminist efforts, that gender is not usually a conscious basis for their decisions.

Reform efforts often involve women who provide the ideas and energy to complement men, but which enable men to dominate the movements. Women generally work in teams to achieve their aims (Mitchell, 1996). Two of the more creative projects described in this chapter are designed by women: Imagine Chicago and the North Carolina Center for Teaching Advancement. The third, the Accelerated Schools project, is designed by a man open to collaboration with projects run by women, such as the Galef Institute. The relationships in educational reform between female leaders and male executives is starting to change, but obvious discrimination has not been confronted.

Though the reform movement in education has given little attention to gender differences, there are explicit efforts to deal with the problems of female students, particularly in encouraging them to enter science and mathematics. Since these fields are dominated by males and male values, individual mentors are effective in providing support and guidance for girls (Mitchell, 1998). Possible relationships and career options that involve life dilemmas described by mentors could be more effectively confronted. Early in their careers, role models provide insight into the thought processes in a particular research field. Female students learn that personal issues remain in flux, as their professional advisors struggle with these issues.

Unlike the Committee for Gender Equity in Calgary, students are not facing the problems of leaders in the reform movement. It would be a giant step for girls to see the ways gender affects women volunteers and staff. There is no evidence of this being done. North American reformers may have to wait for the rest of the world to show them how important the issue of gender is. The aims of reform are dependent on it and the effort to achieve it requires recognition of the women who work to implement change.

PUBLIC DEBATE ABOUT RESULTS

Gender equity is both a result to be achieved as well as an issue involved in the process of change. The intertwining of issues and evaluation is typical of the progress of partnerships. Europeans again anticipated this connection before the Americans began to consider it. Consideration of only educational enrollments and achievements is too narrow, as the case of the Accelerate School Project suggests. Many voluntary organizations suggest measures that relate to the social and individual results that are also involved. The Accelerated Project did not measure the problems of at-risk students, problems of teachers, administrators, and school communities. They favor only studies of students' test results. Alternative measures could include changes in the appearance of the school or the environment of the school landfill, such as suggested by Enviroworks in Chapter 2.

The largest range of different measures are reported mentor programs carried out by non-profit organizations, such as Youth Experiencing Success (National Dropout Prevention Center/Network, n.d.). As discussed in Chapter 3, these programs have many different effects. The results are also impressive. Big Brothers/Big Sisters reports a 46% decrease in drug use and a 37% decline in lying to parents. The Commonwealth Fund shows results from student reports ranging from 62% increase in self-esteem to 35% improvement in family relationships. These variable results can indicate different goals for programs, but the people involved in them (mentors, students, and schools) ought to make these choices.

Placing an issue on the agenda for debate and future action should be a result of evaluations. Leadership Calgary carries out evaluations that are appropriate for other partnerships (2002b). Their surveys find increased scores on a range of questions dealing with the future, organizing for change, and managing change once it is instituted. Other voluntary organizations ask questions that relate to the future of partnerships.

It is often a question of relating a theme to current interests. Arts education benefits from the theory of multiple intelligence more than from research evidence on academic learning resulting from the study of the arts. Currently, small schools are a focus of grants by large foundations, such as the one established by Bill Gates. Rural areas have always had small schools, but they are often characterized as a problem. The failure of Ventures in Education to be linked to the partnership movement or any larger alliance restricts its expansion or emulation.

The issues that are being discussed are as important as the measures of success. For example, the programs that encourage nontraditional career choices by women report attitude changes towards mathematics and science, and attempt to relate changing self-confidence to program participation; both effects are a result of participation in particular programs (McCormick & Wolf, 1993). These programs are aimed at gifted girls, but none is a centerpiece of reform for local and national organizations.

Evaluation is important in education, but measures of success must be interpreted. The measures are often too narrow; neither the aims of the program nor what the project is capable of undertaking are weighed. Europeans are emphasising appropriate social indices for partnerships (Kjaergaard & Wesphalen, 2001). Underdeveloped countries focus on providing schools and having teachers present. In an age of accountability, a preoccupation with test scores on standardized tests of achievement may direct education to a fixed path appropriate for only an earlier factory-based culture.

In contrast, social indicators include the health, welfare, and creative achievements of children, teachers, and community members. For example, schools in the arts show shared concern when the art of teachers as well as students is displayed. Further opportunities for the community in partnerships should enrich the lives of partners as well as those within schools in many parts of the world.

AN ENTREPRENEUR

Those inside the partnership movement see partnerships as critical for the development of education. However, entrepreneurial efforts may be an alternative to partnerships or a basis for partnerships (LaVerne Erickson, presentation for Rural School Principals Program at the University of Calgary, July 31, 2002). Frustrated by the public schools and ways they marginalized the teaching of the arts, Laverne Erickson opened a theater and a private school. In 1973 both activities began in Rosebud, Alberta, Canada, a community of 24 permanent residents. The effort expanded to include a series of independent projects: a passion play in nearby

Drumheller, a program where actors discover if they have talent to perform in Rosebud, a higher education program centered on Vancouver Island in a separate theater, and a placement service for their graduates.

The right to give a higher education certificate required an act of the provincial parliament. Erickson was able to get a private member's bill passed, which is very unusual. The opposition Liberals' attack led the Conservative government to support the bill proposed by one member. Erickson built political alliances when he created his theater. Without large grants, each of these projects is self-sustaining. The theater in Rosebud pays salaries to over 200 people and earns a profit of over $100,000 a year.

These projects are practical and inspirational, which reflects the character of its founder, Laverne Erickson. Mr. Erickson, originally a graduate student at the University of Calgary, received a $5,000 loan from his advisor and bought the building that became the first theater. People have been attracted from over 100 miles to attend Rosebud performances. In the college program, students are taught how to invest their money since artists on average earn less than $12,000 a year. As a result of intelligent and savvy business practices, the Rosebud theater earned 22% on its investment in the difficult markets of 2002.

Problems were converted into opportunities. The passion play encountered opposition because of the division between the town and county in the development of a site for play productions. LaVerne Erickson converted a politician into an actor who played the role of Pontius Pilate. The passion play is the focus for community development in what this charismatic leader calls in a brochure, the Badlands of Canada. The name is meant for Americans who do not understand the geography of their northern neighbor but who know the Badlands in one of their western states. The play and the related developments in nearby communities involve an enormous number of people; most people in Drumheller are involved in the play. The play is to be brought to Israel so that the scenery and costumes could be used twice a year.

Students growing up in Rosebud have a different experience from those growing up in many other rural areas (Mitchell, 2000b). Rural students often are said to receive their high school diploma in one hand and buy their bus ticket to leave the community with the other. Although many people know each other in rural areas, partnerships are fewer than in urban areas. Opportunities require entrepreneurial activities; cultural knowledge can become their capital, such is the case of Europeans in small communities who develop pastry for sale to the cities.

The resources of rural areas are not being sustained. Traditionally, a large number of skilled workers pick up their trades in small towns and rural places (Ibid). However, the computer industry is remote from the rural scene. Rural areas fall further behind each year in terms of computers, internet connections and knowledge of computers. Since 1997, rural schools equal the academic achievement of their city cousins. The schools need to provide the community with the resources for technology and development; technology itself makes it possible for people to live outside urban areas. A strategy for rural areas may include entrepreneurs, partnerships, and community schools. Perhaps LaVerne Erickson is a model for finding beauty, resources, and talent in rural places.

PRIVATE/PUBLIC DIVISIONS

The advocates and implementers of privatization in education highlight the possibilities of entrepreneurial approaches. They argue that innovation would be enhanced by competition with the public system and by the involvement of private firms with schools. Competition with the public system mainly occurs in creating the infrastructure for schools and the support system to maintain them. Schools are increasingly being built by private developers and rented back to the public school system (Luellman, 1997). Indeed, the Canadian province of Nova Scotia is building new schools with only private funds. The British Labour government is following a similar policy.

Bus systems, janitorial services, and specialized teachers, such as in foreign languages, are contracted out by public school systems (David, 1992). If Berlitz teachers are the instructors, the teacher unions have managed to require that certified teachers are also paid. None of these supplementary services are causing a major furor. Charter schools are options within the public system, but they are seen as "private" approaches by their opponents (Mitchell, 2001b). Charter schools are a cause of continuing controversy since they are not controlled by a local school board. When options are available to parents, such as in the voucher systems, the opposition to private efforts is intense.

Partnerships between technological companies and universities reveal how fraught with misunderstanding such partnerships may be (Ginsberg, et al., 2004). Companies, such as Cisco and Nortel, have developed technological certificate programs. One western U.S. university developed a joint program with a Canadian business, which conducted technical training designed to provide its faculty and students with an avenue to a Master's degree at the university.

Both partners tried to increase their market and income. The technological company sought to further train their teachers and students. The university sought to use this program to support further technological advancements in distance education. Without realizing it, both organizations were constrained by divisions within their own institutions. The marketing department failed to involve the teachers in its certificate program, and disappeared in the financial distress experienced by the company. The distance education division was confused by the international evaluation of Canadian students. A Canadian three-year Bachelor's Degree was never accepted for admission. Another unit of the university took half of the tuition credit, although the distance education division did not know this would happen when it signed the Agreement of Understanding with the company.

A "gentlemen's understanding" by representatives of the two institutions failed to clarify important problems. The company treated the university as a company in refusing to advance them expenses, but thought of them as an educational institution who would operate without enough students to pay the instructor. The university treated the company as a unilateral decision maker, guaranteeing them a market, without considering the possibility of the company approaching bankruptcy. The university tried to accommodate students for the company on a quarterly session, rather than on a semester basis. They assumed that one company could provide them with enough students if they met their needs. When the company could not meet its "guess-work" about the numbers of students it would send, the university started to look for other students, such as retired teachers, for this graduate program.

The university failed to see the extent to which the company was subject to market fluctuations and the technological trainers did not consider the university's financial needs. Neither considered the costs of communication and visits between their centers. The university was unable to pass on public funds for marketing to a private company. The company could not arrange for interviews with prospective students as a regular practice in its different locations. Students' interests, including paying in advance and not being reimbursed by the frugal company, were not considered until it was too late. Many of the university's students from the technological company were already in debt and had reached the maximum on their credit cards.

Public schools experience fewer problems when the lines between public and private systems are redrawn. Agencies distribute applications for teachers, although the radical approach of using such agencies to hire teachers is not a practice. The separation of hiring from evaluation is occurring when parents and students become evaluators and schools defend the teachers they have hired. In underdeveloped areas, NGOs are becoming involved with schools to deal with the problem of absentee teachers who make the state schools such an irregular experience for many students (Asia Foundation, n.d.). NGO supported schools are seen by parents in Pakistan as providers of quality education similar to private efforts in richer countries (Rizvi & Sayee, 2004).

In North America, the "mental health" days off by teachers are not seen as a cause for alarm, but the quality of education is an issue for the best students. In the state of Washington, a private company provides advanced placement courses that rural schools could not offer (Mitchell, 1998). Another firm, Ombudsman, takes over the education of at-risk students for whom the public schools' solution is suspension

(David, 1992). Ombudsman provides support and structure for at-risk students with many discipline problems. Private and public efforts outside the school system for drug and health efforts are widely accepted.

Ireland

The development of partnerships may diminish the line between public and private groups. In Ireland, the partnerships make partners into a form of citizenship for individuals. Ireland was becoming the *Celtic Tiger* with the fastest growing Gross Domestic Product in 1987. The Program for National Recovery (PNR) was a program aimed at reducing public deficits (Vestergaard, 2001). As a result of encouragement from the European Union, this budget program included partnership and a decentralized model (Rigney, 2001). This decentralized model encouraged a variety of local partnerships.

In 1996, the original partners of employers, unions, farmers, and government were enlarged by the addition of voluntary and community groups (Vestergaard, 2001). The program includes rural as well as urban communities and attempts to include those that are marginalized from employment, community networks, or decision making. In the depressed town of Limerick, the Catholic Church is involved in an attempt to convert a huge factory (170,000 square feet), the Krups works, into commercial, government service, and community development. Business tenants include a call center and telecommunication firms. Training programs sublct in the project as does the Brothers of Charity.

The Limerick Enterprise Development Partnership (LEDP) is a charitable trust that combines many organizations under the leadership of a small group (Ibid). LEDP includes a network of private businesses, an employers' organization for investing in community development, the municipal corporation, the county council, a state owned company to develop industry and tourism, the city enterprise board, the educational authority, the Catholic diocese, and a pre-existing partnership to eliminate poverty.

The closing of the Krups plant led a small group to develop a common plan, although one businessperson played a key role. The tight team that manages LEDP includes the business initiator, the manager, and financial manager. The team has become strong enough for one of the original key supporters to be replaced without difficulty.

The Limerick project, similar to other local ones, exceeds any expectations of the central Irish government. LEDP has created over 300 jobs and training positions (Ibid). The different perspectives of the various players converge. Government representatives see the businesspeople as having strong social commitments while those on the business side see the public authorities involved in LEDP as efficient. The variety of members mobilizes support for the project and its continuation. The informal meetings of LEDP add to their plans, including the creation of an adult education center.

In spite of many successful local projects, the Irish government itself has not developed alternatives. Unlike the continent of Europe, union and management partnerships remain exceptions (European Foundation for the Improvement of Living and Working Conditions, 1997). Linking local policies to national efforts would improve the progress of minorities. Employment of women has doubled as the economic miracle occurs in Ireland. All minorities and the partnership program itself are challenged by economic depressions.

MARGINALITY

Creative partnerships arise from efforts of societies, such as those in Ireland, or organizations, such as the Gender Equity program at the Calgary School Board. Such partnerships are unfortunately marginal to the dominant societies, organizations, or governments. For most educators, particularly in Canada, any discussion of private efforts is not yet legitimate; they insist on maintaining their monopoly. Most of the projects discussed in this chapter are the direct result of creative people seeing different ways of confronting problems or possibilities. Leadership Calgary, Image Chicago, the Accelerated Schools, and the Rosebud theater are the results of insightful individuals.

If students challenge the authority of schools, they are beyond the pale and are unlikely to share in the developing partnerships. At-risk students are the objects of partnerships discussed in this chapter and in Chapter 2. Subordination creates problems rather than possible innovations. Borders of organizations can be breached only when the boundary spanners can mount the ladders.

The most significant partnerships allow all participants to express themselves. Inclusion of marginal individuals means a rejection of planning for them. People in between institutions are more important to study for the future rather than successful businesspeople or professionals of today. Arts partners, questionable community activists, or students at-risk are the partners at the edge of today's culture. Such individuals can do more than react to conflict; they can create cultural alternatives.

In order to break new ground, creative engineers and scientists need the support provided by daily contact with superiors; without the supervisor's support, new ideas are often destroyed by criticism from peers (Mitchell, 1971). Similarly, creative writing in an elementary school may resemble a "witch hunt" because of the negative criticism from other students (Henry, 1965). Revealingly, creative scientists have a variety of friends with different ideas, but their closest friends support their own position (Pelz, 1957).

The inclusion of marginal people allows for possible new partnerships and opportunities for existing alliances. Partnerships may overextend themselves by adding more members' groups, as discussed in Chapter 4. In this chapter, we find partnerships limited by their focus on their own alumni, narrow tasks, or test results. Partnerships require organizational direction for national or humanistic causes. In a federal system or council of partnerships, local partnerships may contribute to a larger, perhaps international, organization.

Creative partnerships evolve into an international program or one with a variety of constituents. As the case of Ireland suggests, partnerships are a new alternative that builds a community of active citizens. Measures of success become a process that people themselves use to guide actions, rather than a tool used by experts to measure others. In determining goals, international comparisons suggest further options. The experience of Irish partnerships indicates that the involvement of churches in partnerships could go beyond the activities of churches as social service organizations, discussed in Chapter 4. The wider network of partnerships should also diminish the bias from the dominance of only one type of partner. The variety of partners may, in turn, surpass the independence of experts in providing secure evaluations. The vitality of partnership requires a combination of national and local efforts, private and public engagements, and established and marginal players; they are creating the puzzle, not just solving it.

Chapter 6: New Options

Would you tell me, please, which way I ought to go from here? That depends
a good deal on where you want to get to, said the Cat (L. Carroll, 1992, p. 76)

All partnerships are capable of adding to the repertoire of educators. Artists and
scientists add directly to teaching, but other partners may add to the organization of
education, if not the curriculum. Specific groups of students, teachers, and
administrators may be involved in the development of partnerships. If such
partnerships include too many groups they risk becoming unmanageable. Financial
masters, such as foundations, may create dependency so that partnerships only pursue
funding. The educational contribution of partnerships should be paramount, but the
work in which they are involved remains on the margins of educational practice
(Black, 2004).

The constituents of partnerships need help if they are to develop further within
partnerships. Planning for partnerships can be enhanced through awareness of the
differences among types of partnership. The efforts of artists, business, science, and
community groups can become complementary. Different cultures also bring out
other possible contributions. For example, Americans stress local efforts while
Europeans aim to develop regions. Partnerships can reverse the position and
perspective of those involved in education. When partnerships link with other groups
experiencing more difficulties than themselves, they can become concerned about
more than their own "sustainability." Internationally, countries in the South can help
their more affluent partners to enhance education by showing, for example, the
continuing importance of gender inequality.

Educators can appreciate social goals as well as academic achievements when
working with students, particularly at-risk youths. Diversity within education
depends on finding and supporting marginality among individuals, schools and

cultures. Change often requires reverse approaches, such as enriching the education of at-risk students.

STUDENTS

Viewing partnership through comparative lenses reveals new opportunities for students that can be enhanced by cooperation among partners. At-risk students particularly benefit from the efforts of business, science, and the arts acting separately, but they could gain even more by the coordination of these diverse partners. Universities are in a position to show how cooperation with community groups benefits marginal students. Greater inclusion of marginal youths is possible when universities and schools work together as they do in the Ventures in Education program. European partnerships explicitly focus community efforts on at-risk youths, including immigrants and special education students.

Many celebrations of success provide opportunities to relate different types of partnerships to at-risk students. Celebrations might set goals for student leaders and provide for their greater involvement. Cooperation among student leaders and educational administrators shows how power must be understood and used for the benefit of students. Separate voices for students through independent newspapers makes this connection possible.

A balance between specialized leaders and generalized roles is necessary. Invidious comparisons among professional specialists stand in contrast to cooperation that volunteers are able to develop. The volunteers are becoming more specialized and the educational experts ought to reveal more concern about people. The student role has been assumed to be a foreshadowing of future general leadership, but it is possible to include varied positions.

Conditions influencee the type of leadership required for any group. Competition and limited resources promote tangible partnerships, but general efforts require commitment and vision by the leaders involved. Emergency situations result in attracting the most appropriate combination of leaders. The emergency corps in Western Australia and the use of research by students working with Stanford

University both reveal new roles for student leaders.

VOLUNTEERS

Women manage most partnerships in ways compatible with a volunteer role (Mitchell, 2000a). Women, who are teachers, parents, or executives for NGOs, create opportunities for interaction among themselves to guide tight groups in their efforts to partnnerships. An example is Dr. Mary Schmidt, who coordinates a school's art education program, in spite of her busy medical schedule Men are increasingly involved as community members, while both genders are often able to support voluntary efforts when they retire.

The established organizations, such as the PTA, provide few additional opportunities to involve women or others who are immersed in their careers. Community volunteers provide an alternative to specialized middle management who are so career orientated that they frequently are unable to cooperate among themselves for the community. Retirees are the main reservoir of potential volunteers. Partnerships require the "thank-God- for-people" who are concerned about the partnership whether they are volunteers or employees (Hughes, 1958).

LEADERS

Major changes require a transformation of leadership to integrate partnerships for the benefit of students. Such leaders scan the boundaries for original opportunities and search for additional alternatives and directions for joint activities. When partnerships move beyond two groups contributing their separate resources, leaders with long-term vision are needed to develop the multiple relationships. The integration of organizing and planning as contributions to an educational sequence calls for the establishment of a leadership group. These groups have complementary members, such as in South Carolina, where state institutions of art, education and universities support each other's resources and roles.

Partnerships may exceed the capacity of leaders to incorporate new elements. Change in the leadership group often ends a partnership or prevents its development; two or more levels are needed to overcome these problems. Federated systems of partnerships remove some of the instability provoked by separate and conflicting partnerships. The systematic addition of new partner representatives and new ways of linking local efforts to broader ones may provide a way of renewing the educational aims of partnerships. There is no real necessity for every partnership to rediscover itself. Within a federation, variety can nourish creativity. Overcoming the institutional differences between partners, such as business and higher education, could be the first step in creating partnerships with vision. A policy for federations requires multiple aims to match the variety of its constituents.

r. u. MAD?

In Australia a coalition of foundations has been organized to change both the attitudes of foundations and the culture of young people (Black, 2004). This initiative, r.u.MAD? (Are You Making A Difference?) asks young people to improve their communities. It was started by the Stegley Foundation, a progressive philanthropic trust, which, in 1997, decided to terminate its trust and spend all its resources by 2001. Like sunset legislation where all the laws and regulations are suspended after a fixed date unless there is a new reason for their existence, terminating the foundation challenged the trustees to find the grant with the best returns rather than following the usual and safe procedures. The Stegley Foundation decided to focus on the answers that young people would have to Australian social problems and to develop their volunteer roles.

r.u.MAD? represents a definitive movement away from the traditional model of sponsorship towards strategic philanthropy. This new model defines itself as a community capacity-building strategy that emphasizes action with a real and lasting impact, instead of quick-fix solutions that do not address underlying social needs. Strategic philanthropy assumes a two-way flow of benefits and outcomes through the sharing of ideas and resources, not all of which need to be monetary.

r.u.MAD? is a new model of philanthropy that teaches young people to value the three T's: "time, talent or abilities, and 'treasure' or useful physical resources." It involves capacity building where students seek long-term answers to community needs. It involves a sharing between students and the community, rather than an attempt to fix student needs. Its focus is on social action to which social studies in school might contribute, but understanding of society is developed through action.

r.u.MAD? projects are developed by the students for local problems and lead to partnerships between schools and communities. By July 2002, 60 schools were involved in the program. Neither schools nor professionals receive grants separately from students. Grants are made for professional development and curriculum resources that will make learning realistic. The aim is to enhance the ability of students to make decisions, work with others, and become leaders. This program sees students as a capital investment for society that can return benefits for their community in the future.

The challenge for r.u. MAD? is to find ways to link students to broad, lasting partners in Australia and the world. The sponsors have attempted to find alliances with other foundations in Australia and the United States (Black, 2004). The Foundation brokered a wide number of partnerships between philanthropic trusts, foundations, independent philanthropists and peak bodies. In Australia, the original Stegley Foundation was joined by Education Foundation, Myer Foundation, William Buckland Foundation and Paul Edward Dehnert Trust. Similar activities are being developed with the Change Foundation in San Francisco.

The aim of projects like this one is to develop a new kind of school for a different future where community partnerships flow from roots in the local community. Maverick leaders are supported, particularly at the secondary level, as a result of this project. The community, not the curriculum, becomes the driving force while partnerships are central to the direction of schools. Students are given experience in developing long-term activities, unlike current demands of classrooms where they respond only to unrelated and daily demands.

In developing projects for students, leaders must look in two directions for all members of their coalitions: planning for the future and solving immediate problems. The vision of leaders stretches towards international levels but also includes student leaders in local efforts. Leaders frame a learning community that includes students, parents, community members, and teachers. Social and medical services provide an opportunity for schools to widen their function at home while assessing the needs of those abroad. Educational alternatives can develop together with public policies.

ALTERNATIVES

Partnerships encourage learning and different approaches to achieve greater success in schools. The perspective of Europeans shows how important national and regional conferences are in suggesting directions for partnerships. Europeans are more experienced and move steadily towards closing the barriers between private and public organizations. Voluntary or non-profit organizations make these connections possible. Concern for student inequalities has emerged in Europe as has the view from Ireland that partnerships are a new corollary of citizenship. These visions may involve international efforts that federated councils are able to promote.

North American partnerships should be concerned about inequalities and the resources that NGOS are able to mobilize to deal with them. Foundations are an important new resource for multiple partnerships, but their instability can create problems for partnerships that are not financially and structurally independent. In less developed countries, foundations, donor countries, and NGOs attempt together to overcome poverty. In all countries religion is an important resource in reaching people if it is possible to avoid competition among religions or constitutional arguments about such relationships.

After being separated for over a hundred years, the division between religion and schools is being removed in the United States. Social services provided by religious groups is the major addition to the relationship between state and schools. The practices of religion, including meaningful rituals, are not yet appreciated, but they could contribute to greater stability of partnerships. Whether in community service or business, celebrations of success are being rediscovered. However, rituals to transform students and link them to partnerships are still an exceptional occurrence. Rituals may also be the means whereby partners are effectively integrated. Modern urban schools tend to eliminate rituals, such as opening-day ceremonies.

IMAGINATIVE REVERSALS

There are many other divisions besides the separation of religion and education that partnerships should overcome. r.u.MAD has suggested how this process can occur. These compartments to be integrated include: overcoming the schism between gifted and at-risk students, the separation of roles for men and women in social movements, the division between private and public lines in schooling, and the opposition between grass-roots efforts by one partnership to the organization of a national partnership policy.

A continuing means for overcoming these polarities is required. The activities that initiate partnerships suggest that these initial steps should be constantly renewed. Through boundary spanning, leaders could continue to find solutions from different groups in a variety of locations. In order to work between organizations, small tight groups need to be multiplied across organizations. Top leaders form such groups easily, but the specialization and single administrative setting of middle leaders mean that they must be rewarded for experience outside their own organization before they can become supporters of partnerships. Partnerships can provide a basis for both levels of administrators to widen their approach to represent the community and become leaders of broader domains.

Polarities among partners and interests require separate organizations to develop heterogeneous goals themselves. Companies are discovering that they must be responsive to ethnic, gender, and group interests. Variety within schools can similarly be supported by different approaches. Complementary individuals become the most important partners. The matching of students with partners throughout the development of youths is the essential action in order to link partnerships. The variety of allies could, in turn, lead to approaches to education that focus on different types of students or programs.

Exchanges of students across schools and between communities provide a direct educational meaning to partnership. A number of such partnerships are forming between suburban and inner city schools (Northeastern Illinois University, 1994). Future partnerships could connect rural schools with urban ones and those with similar programs across great distances. Partnerships are for students and should involve them as separate leaders, as well as links to administrators.

Imaginative attempts must go beyond current partnership practices. Leadership programs increasingly expose administrators to learning in cooperation with community groups. Appreciation theory leads to viewing the best people and practices as models for others in society and for framing future options. Limited current approaches could be replaced by alternatives. Narrow professional education should yield to humane and liberal learning. A preoccupation with standards and measurement ought to be extended to include social indicators that people have chosen themselves to guide their actions if they are to realize their potential. Particularly because their evaluation efforts are broader, voluntary organizations often have valuable perspectives to supplement the views of educators. They can suggest ways schools can measure results for improving the lives of students, families, and communities.

It is important to see that current concerns are not the only problems. Measurement may include more than subject and ability tests. In the case of the Accelerated School Project, social indicators would provide a basis for developing cohesion within the project if it continues to be open to outside organizations. The provision for the development of internal standards and opportunities for outsiders to contribute is a necessary and fundamental goal of all parnerships. Internal advocacy groups, such as the gender effort in Calgary, would be a useful source for such initiatives. Internal groups are particularly able to distinguish between official positions and the way reality is.

Partnerships involve many issues, such as the private and public divisions, which universities, governments and schools are all facing. Partnerships everywhere may require other approaches, such as entrepreneurship, as a supplement. Schools may see the value of teaching investing to students aiming for careers that will not be financially rewarding, such as the arts. Businesses might find how much they can learn about networking from schools that developed such links or social agencies that found ways of providing for people with special needs. Educational programs become resources that rural communities or declining neighborhoods need to define their futures. The range of options is increased by consideration of alternatives to present policies and positions asere partnerships are further developed.

MARGINALITY AS A RESOURCE

These ideas about marginality have been influential in the study of many occupations and community groups, including artists (Mitchell, 2000a). In most of these studies, members of one occupation attempt to join another field, or are trapped between two occupations. For example, students in arts education are often caught between the fine arts and commercial arts. It is the experience of being separated from almost all others, particularly society's elite that is most critical for developing the outsider perspective.

However, the most extensive use of the marginality concept is in the study of immigrants; indeed, the idea originates in ethnic studies (Mitchell, 2000a). 'Marginality' is part of the attempt to clarify the conduct of immigrants who dissociate themselves from their original group and, at the same time, attempt to join representatives of the dominant culture. Unsuccessful in these efforts, the marginal person lives on the edge of both worlds. Aboriginals are often said to be "red on the outside and white on the inside." The marginality concept embraces the diverse behaviour of the parvenu, the migrant, and the deracinated.

The broad interactions among business, science, the arts, and social service would be limited according to the original formulation of marginality. Business and science have a higher status, while the arts and social service suffer from a stigma of being less rewarded in our society and associated with academic disciplines that are not well established. Partnerships in a fringe area are particularly likely to be abandoned or viewed as being less important by teachers and administrators who are not involved. Schools are influenced by these many partners as well as hundreds of other innovators (Mitchell, 1998). Furthermore, unless partnerships contribute directly to teaching a subject or grade, all partnerships are marginal to staff not directly involved in the process of change. We can see marginality as a set of positive options.

REVIEW

In our companion book, *Worldwide Partnerships for Schools with Voluntary Organizations, Foundations, Universities, Companies and Community Council (2004)* Patricia Klinck presents a reflective review. I have quoted her "Afterword" in order to comment for my summary.

> The focus of this book has been on the development of international partnerships so that students – regardless of location, age or stage of their lives – can lead richer lives. In each case, the vision and goals go beyond what can be accomplished 'alone'. Searching for like-minded people is key to each journey and its successes (p. 283).

Finding this common ground is ironically dependent upon marginal people. Metis leaders develop partnerships because of their ability to see connections as shown in our Chapter 1. It is important to find people in situations who continually perceive alternatives and act upon them. People who often behave in unexpected ways, whether students, volunteers or leaders, are regarded as marginal by most people in society. Marginality also draws attention to the tentative relationship between individuals and society. Individuals may not be completely assimilated into groups or the groups may be separated from the rest of society. Marginal people remain in-between. Partnerships provide opportunities for them to come together to share reflections and to enrich their lives and those of many ohers.

> The subtext of each chapter is part of an old human story. As in the legends and fables of old, a few set out to change the world, to discover a new way of being, a new order. They can see the potential to change things. They see the gap between what is and what could be. Like Martin Luther King, they have a dream. These dreams, the need to make a difference is at the heart of partnerships. It does not – indeed cannot – go smoothly. The undertaking is huge and it depends upon good will and cooperation. It is what some philosophers have called a 'loving struggle'. Not everyone is prepared to undertake such a journey (Ibid).

The goals for partnerships may be either liberal or radical, such as ensuring a greater degree of equality in schools or a return to tradition, including links with religion. Partnerships are a specific form of creativity that enhances education and culture. Those who develop partnerships are often able to see limits of the current systems. At-risk students can link with retirees who are able to understand and relate to their experiences. Women who maintain voluntary organizations should also be provided with opportunities to become leaders together with men in order to develop their different leadership styles. The focus on at-risk students requires the combined guidance and assistance of both genders.

Religion is an unlikely source for modern partnerships since it is a source of resistance to globalization and dogma. However, connecting schools with religion may bring positive results. Religion is the original integrating service, but even its role in dealing with death is challenged by counselors. It is ironical that social and medical services should be combined in schools without religion. It is increasingly recognized that the force of ritual is needed to support students who are currently involved in partnerships and that churches may provide more than supplementary after-school programs. Religion may be appreciated in the future for its ability to connect peoples and varied ideas, the aim of partnerships.

It is clear in each case that the goals for change are not accompanied by 'true' answers. Who knows what is needed for remote villagers? Who dares give the definitive statement on literacy? What does it mean to live in 'peace'? As the partners work in these intractable 'problems', they call on their alliances and colleagues. They develop cross disciplinary networks to find greater creativity. The new world they are trying to create is accompanied by complexities and ambiguity. At times a burden, this uncertainty can -and does - give rise to complex intricate 'solutions and perspectives'. Sometimes ideas and processes combine in new ways. Sometimes the solution has always been there but has gone unseen until 'new eyes' refocus and it comes out as being good. What is evident in those fleeting insights is that the 'solution' cannot be replicated in another context. The 'solution' lies in the close collaboration of the partners - the uncounted and unrecorded hours spent. They had to seize the opportunities. Success appears to depend upon certain key concepts: principles of collaboration, allies and truth sayers, renegades who push the boundaries of the taken for granted, etc. Perhaps even more it depends upon good will, trust and hope, accompanied by lively critical debate. These are elements that take time and form differently in each context (284).

Partnerships become as productive as their constituent members become. The development of people within partnerships is critical. Educators are discovering the value of community involvement in professional development education. Professional groups need to sense the value of recognizing youth within their in-service education and regular programs. Presentations by youth and artistic performances can be a way of illustrating professional themes, providing an alternative way of learning, and a more imaginative break than simply coffee breaks. For example, elementary students made such contributions to the Rural School Principals Program at the University of Calgary. Partnerships can transform school practices and the curriculum when these activities, like others in our society, are seen as needing all the creativity we can muster to make changes.

> What is obvious is that partnerships are newly developing relationships that produce something unique which neither individuals nor organizations would produce on their own. Their success depends on reciprocity and a common purpose, a common weal. These stories are essentially moral tales. In my mind's eye, I see the partners sitting late at night, on email, on the phone in deep conversations, committed to taking the steps necessary to make a difference in the lives of those for whom they advocate.

Work on partnerships has been hampered by assuming that partnerships are all cut from the same cloth. Partnerships are multicolored cloaks with many different types of materials. Underdeveloped countries are discovering them as an alternative to government and official agencies. Developed countries are concerned about the stability of partnerships when they should be focused upon introducing change in their rigid systems built for a different era and another set of purposes. Partnerships can provide both types of countries with a basis for developing civic responsibility, particularly when such cases as Ireland, are dramatized. The stories of partnerships are accounts, in an international context, for local adaptation.

Are there moments when such dreams appear? Or are they born of intuition and some other unknown elements? We can see that in some cases the 'marker' event was a conference theme, in others it was a chance meeting, in others it was a cataclysmic event such as a war. In all cases, fellow travelers come together to begin the journey. Sometimes they come from unexpected locations, other times from nearby. In all cases there is much talk - a testing of the values, the vision, the capacity to work together. Partnerships form and inform the project and the participants in unexpected ways. At times, the going is smooth. But as they cross over borders, enter new territory, challenges and complexities loom out of the chimera. In response, they seek out resources: kindred souls, other organizations, grants, funding, political support. They stay open to chance meetings, serendipity, new counsel and advice. Sometimes they change course, take a different tack, learn from cautionary tales and the mistakes of others. Sometimes their partnership is solid but the organizations to which they are affiliated are not flexible. They work at changing policy, outcomes and whatever is necessary to succeed. Over time some partnerships change their focus, adapt to new contexts and potential. They develop in ways that the founders could never have envisaged. Other times they fail (Ibid).

Bibliography

Alt, M. & Medrich, E. (1994). Student outcomes from participation in community service. Paper prepared for the U. S. Department of Education by MPR Associate [On-line]. Available: http://www.quest.edu/ slaricle13.html.

Above and Beyond (2001-2002, Winter). Newsletter for advisors and student leaders across Canada. *Above and Beyond*, 5(2), 1-5.

Above and Beyond (2002, Spring). Newsletter for advisors and student leaders across Canada. *Above and Beyond*, 5(3), 1-6.

Anderson, J. (1998). Service-learning and teacher education. *ERIC Digest* (ED421481).

Anderson, V. (1998, February). Art advocates seek to prove arts' value. *Catalyst* [On-line). Available: fel:///Cl/ricky/temp/whyart.htm.

Appreciative Inquiry Commons (n.d.). *Outstanding cases: A Chicago case of intergenerational appreciative inquiry* [On-line]. Available: wysiwyg://75 /http:// appreciativeinquiry.cwru. edu/intro/bestcases.

Asia Foundation (n.d.). *Lessons from public-private partnerships: The education sector in Pakistan* [On-line]. Available: www.abbi.org/pdf/partnerships/ secondprinting/19asiafound.pdg.

Associated Press (2002, July 10). Foundations yank funding to Pittsburgh schools. *CNN News* [On-line]. Available:wysiiwyg://http://fyi.cnn.com/ 20002/fyi/...ws/07/10/ pittsburgh.schools.ap/index.html.

Bank of America (1995, April 1). *The Orr school network a community-based educational partnership 1989–1995.* Chicago: Bank of America.

Barnett, R. & Blumner, J. (1999). *Writing centers and writing across the curriculum programs.* Westport, CT: Greenwood Press.

Belsie, L. (2001, September 13). 'Look for what's right.' *Christian Science Monitor* [On-line]. Available: http://www.csmonitor.com/2001/0913/p15sl-lihc.html.

Berman, E.H. (1989). The state's stake in educational reform. In Shea, C.M., Kahane, E., & Sola, P. (Eds.), *The new servants of power* (pp. 57-66). New York: Greenwood Press.

Black, R. (2004). Thinking community as a social investment in Australia. In Mitchell, S., Klinck, P., & Burger, J. (Eds). *Worldwide partnerships for schools with voluntary organizations, foundations, universities, companies, and community councils* (pp. 223-252). Lewiston, NY: Edwin Mellen.

Bleich, M. (1996). Revisionism and reform. *Education Week*, [On-line]. Available: http://Edweek.org/ew/ewstory.cfm?ibleich.h15.

Bloom, H., Ham, S., Melton, L., & O'Brien (2001). *Evaluating the Accelerated Schools approach* [On-line]. Available: htt://www.mdrc.org/ Reports2001/

AcceleratedSchools/AccSchools.htm.

Blum, J., (2000, May 26). Scores are up in D.C. Schools, *Washington Post*, B1.

Bodinger-deUriarte. C., McCormick, T., Schwager, M. Danzberger, J. & Clark, M. (1996). *A guide to promising practice in educational partnerships.* Available: ed.gov/pubs/PromPract/index.html.

Boyd, W. (Trans. & Ed.). (1956). *The Emile of Jean Jacques Rousseau Selections.* New York: Teachers College.

Bradley, A. (1989, November 15). After 10 years, idea-sharing network links teachers in 31 states, districts. *Education Week* [On-line]. Available: http://EDweek.org (archives).

Brousseau, C. (1999, February 6). Harmonious Partnership. *Kingston Whig Standard*, Companion section, pp. 1, 3.

Brown, B. (1998). Service learning: More than community service. *ERIC DIGEST*, No. 198 (ED421640).

Brown, D (1995). *School with heart: Voluntarism and public education.* Vancouver: Faculty of Education, University of British Columbia.

Business Week (1989, Winter). Cities in Schools. *Business Week*, Special Advertising Section.

Calgary Board of Education (2003, September 30). Partners in learning [On-line]. Available : http://www.cbe.ab.ca/ch_supt/partnerships.

Canadian Broadcasting System (1994). *Community and its counterfeits.* Toronto: CBC Radio Works.

Carroll, L. (1992). *Alice's adventures in wonderland.* New York: Alfred A. Knopf.

Cavanagh, S. (2002, August 7). Leaving Las Vegas schools. *Education Week, 21(43)m 40-46,*

Chicago Association of Local School Councils (1995). *Construction ahead... LSC at work.* Chicago: Chicago Association of Local School Councils.

Clark, R. (1988). School-university relationships: An interpretative review. In Sironik, K. & Goodlad, J. (Eds.) *School-university partnerships in action* (pp. 32-65). New York: Teachers College, Columbia University.

Clark, R. (1996). *Art education in postmodernist pedagogy.* Reston, Virginia: Canadian Society for Education through Art and National Art Education Association.

Clearinghouse on Educational Management, College of Education, University of Oregon (n.d.). *Trends and issues: Relationships with the community*, [On-line]. Available: http://www:///ERIC.uoregan.edu/trends-jsshes/relat/03.html.

Cobb, C. & Rixford, C. (1998). *Lessons learned from the history of social indicators.* San Francisco: Redefining Progress.

The Collaborative (2001). *Accelerated Schools Project* [On-line}. Available: http://www:ctlonline.org/ programs/programs_asp.asp.

Communities in Schools (1996). *Building community to help kids stay in school 1996 Annual Report.* Alexandria, Virginia: Authors.

Communities in Schools (2001). *A year of connections, relationships and results.*

Alexandria, VA: Authors.

Community Foundations of Canada (2001). *Principles for Community Foundations.* Ottawa: Community Foundations of Canada.

Cooperrider, D. & Whitney, D. (n.d.). *A positive revolution in change: Appreciative inquiry* (Draft) [On-line]. Available: wysiwyg://82/http:// appreciativeinquiry. cwru.edu.

Copenhagen Centre (1999). *New employment partnerships in Europe.* Copenhagen: Copenhagen Centre.

Cortes, E. (n.d.). Reweaving the fabric: The iron rule and the IAF strategy for dealing with poverty and politics. Austin: Texas Industrial Areas Foundation Network.

Council for Aid to Education (1994). *Business/education organizations: roles and opportunities to work together.* New York: Council for Aid to Education.

Covallis School District 509J, Oregon State University & Hewlett Packard (n.d.). *Science Education Partnterships* [On-line]. Available:http://www.septs.org. whatis.htm.

Corporate-Higher Education Forum (1987). *From patrons to partners.* Montreal: Corporate-Higher Education Forum.

DareArts Foundation (2001). *Annual Report.* Caledon East, On: DareArts.

David, A. (1992). *Public-private partnerships: The private sector and innovation in education* [On-line]. Available: http://www.rppi.org/education/ps142.html.

Davis, M. (2002, June 19). New Ed. Dept. office reaches out to the faithful. *Education Week,* 21(41), pp. 15, 28.

DiPeso, J. (n.d.). Religion and the environment [On-line]. Available: http://www.lightparty.com/Economic /ReligionAndEnvironment.html.

Dixon, N. (2002, June 21). Chicago seeks soldiers for schools. *Washington Post.* On-line: wysiwyg://9/http: //www.washingtonpost.com.

Eckert, P. (1989). *Jocks & burnouts.* New York: Teachers College Press.

Education Week (1999). *IMPACT II* [On-line]. Available: http://www. edweek. org/context/orgs/i22.html.

El Ansari, W. (2004). Incentives for partnerships and subsequent difficulties. In Mitchell, S., Klinck, P., & Burger, J. (Eds.) *Worldwide partnerships for schools with voluntary organizations, foundations, universities, companies, and community councils* (pp. 191-222).

Epstein, A. (2002, January 30). Bush's Un-American and immoral call for "national service." *MediaLink Ann Rand Institute* [On-line]. Available: http:// www.aynrand. org/medialink.

European Commission Education (1999). *Indicators and benchmarks of quality of school education* [On-line]. Available http://europa.eu.int/comm/education/ indic/indic1cn.html.

European Foundation for the Improvement of Living and Working Conditions (1998). *Management-union partnerships are rare in Ireland* [On-line]. Available: wysiwyg://5/http://www.eiro.eurofound.ie/1998/07/featur3e/

IE9807120F.html.

Faulstick, B. (2002, April 8). Program helping valley cut dropout rate. *Las Vegas Review-Journal* [On-line]. Available: http://www.lvrj-home/2002/Apr-08-Mon-2002/ 18444641.html.

Follett, M. (1973). *Dynamic administration: The collected papers of Mary Parker Follett*, edited by E. Fox & L. Urwick. London: Pittman.

Foote, C., Battaglia, C., & Vermette, P. (1999). A partnership for the future of secondary education in Niagara Falls, N. Y. Paper presented to American Educational Research Association.

Foss, K. (2002, July 12). Living together a popular first step, data show. *Globe and Mail*, p. 1, 10.

Fowler, J. (1991). *A guide for building an alliance for science, mathematics and technology education.* College Park, MD: Triangle Coalition for Science and Technology Education.

Freethought Today (2000, April). Church-school "partnerships" decried [On-line]. Available: htt:// www.ffrf.org.fttoday/april2000/partnerships.html.

Freedman, M. (1994). *Seniors in national and community service.*
Philadelphia: Public/Private Ventures.

Gardner, J. (1990). *On learning.* New York: Free Press.

Gaskell, J., Binkley, N., Nicoll, C., & McLaughlin, K. (1995). *The arts as an equal partner: The story of Langley Fine Arts School.* Toronto: Canadian Education Association.

Ginsberg, R., Davies, T. & Quick, D. (2004). A North American public-private higher education partnership. In Mitchell, S., Klinck, P., & Burger, J. (Eds) *Worldwide partnerships for schools with voluntary organizations, foundations, universities, companies, and community councils* (pp. 3-32). Lewiston, NY: Edwin Mellen.

Goertz, M. (2001, September). Refining government roles in an era of standards-based reform. *Phi Delta Kappan*, 83(1), 62-66.

Government of Ontario, Minister of Citizenship (2001). *High school involvement program* [On-line]. Available:http://www.gov.on.ca/mczer/english/citdiv/voluntar/involve.htm.

Graham, P. (1992). *S. O. S. Sustain our schools. New York: Hill & Wang.*

Gribben, C., Pinnington, K., & Wilson, A. (2000). *Government as partners.* Copenhagen: Copenhagen Centre.

Hall, O. & Carlton, R.. (1977). *Basic skills at school and work.* Toronto: Ontario Economic Council.

Harris, M. (1987). *The arts at Black Mountain College.* Cambridge, MA: MIT Press.

Havighurst, R. (1964). *The public schools of Chicago.* Chicago: Chicago Public Schools.

Henry, J. (1965). *Culture against man.* New York: Random House.

Hewton, E. (1982). *Rethinking educational change.* Guildfor, Sussex: Society for

Research into Higher Education.

Hiebert, B. (2004). Comments: Systems and individuals. In Mitchell, S., Klinck P., & Burger, J. (Eds.) *Worldwide partnerships for schools with voluntary organizations, foundations, universities, companies, and community councils* (pp. 80-82). Lewiston, NY: Edwin Mellen.

Hoff, D. (2001, November 7). NSF plots new education strategy. *Education Week*, 21(10), pp. 1, 20, 21.

Hopfenberg, W. Levin, H., Chase, C., Christensen, S., Moore, M., Soler, P., Brunner, I., Keller, B. & Rodriguez, C. (1993). San Francisco: Jossey-Bass.

Howe, I. (1966). *Steady Work: Essays in the politiics of democratic radicalism, 1953-1966.* New York: Harcourt Brace.

Hughes, E. (1958). *Men and their work.* New York: The Free Press.

Human City Institute (2001). *Ten years of Imagine Chicago* [On-line]. Available: http://www.humancity.org.

Huskins, B. (1999, November). Teaching the parents; Educating the kids. *Leadership Calgary Newsletter* [On-line]. Available; htt:://www.volunteer calgary... leadershipCalgary/archives/9922newsletter.html.

Ihejirika, M. (2000, March). Imagine Chicago, Depaul 6 museums, 7 schools-- Bingo! *Catalyst* [On-line]. Available: http://catalyst-chicago.org/03-00/0300 imagine.html.

Immerwehn, J., Johnson, J., & Kernan-Schloss, A. (1992). *Cross talk: the public, the experts, and competitiveness.* Washington, D.C.: Business-Higher Education Forum.

Imagine Chicago (2001). *About Imagine Chicago* [On-line]. Available: http://imaginechicago.org/about-us.html.

Institute for Community Development and the Arts (1996). *Building America's communities.* Washington, D. C.: National Assembly of Local Arts Agencies.

Intel Corporation (2002). Accelerated Schools collaborates with Intel Corporation [On-line]. Available: http://www.sp.ucom.edu/~wwwasp/news/ volume11/no 1oage3_4_4html.

Kallick, J. & Jobs for the Future (1990). *Voices from school and home.* Sommerville, MA: Jobs for the Future.

Kjaergaard, C. & Westphalen, S. (Eds.) (2001). *From collective bargaining to social partnerships: New roles of the social partners in Europe.* Copenhagen: Copenhagen Centre.

Jacobson, L. (2002, May 1). The little scientists. *Education Week*, 21(33), pp. 28-33.

Jacobson, L. (2004, January 21) Students bring youthful perspective to state ed. boards. *Education Week*, 23(19), p. 8.

Jacobsen, M. & Gladston, B. (2002). From project within a school to provincial network. In Mitchell, S. (Ed.). *Effective educational partnerships* (pp. 43-62) Westport, CT: Praeger.

Jacobsen, M. & Gladstone, B. (2004). Education reform meets NetMedia. In Mitchell, S., Klinck, P., & Burger, J. (Eds). *Worldwide partnerships for schools with voluntary organizations, foundations,universities,companies, and community councils* (pp. 33-63). Lewiston, NY: Edwin Mellen.

Kennedy Y. E. L. L. Project (2002). *Y. E. L. L. Project and Youth Report.* Standford, CA: John W. Gardner for Youth and Their Communities.

John W. Gardiner Center for Youth and Their Communities (2001). *A Handbook for Supporting Community Youth Researchers [On-line].* Available: http://gardnercenter.standord.edu/resources/handbook.

Johnson, J. (1999, December). Youth vision. *Leadership Calgary Newsletter* [On-line]. Available htt::://www.volunteercalgary...rshipCalgary/archives/9912 newletter.html.

Joyce, B. & Calhoun, E. (1996). *Learning experiences in school renewal.* Eugene, Oregon: Clearinghouse on Educational Management, University of Oregon.

Kenan Best Practices Center (n.d.). *Welcome to the Kenan Best Practices Center* [On-line]. Available: http://BestPractices.ga.unc.edu.

Knowles, J. (1973). *The Rockefeller financial group.* Andover, Massachusetts: Warner Modular.

Kristensen, J. (2001). Corporate social responsibility and new social partnerships. In Kjaergaard, C. & Wesphalen, S. (Eds.) *From collective bargaining to social partnerships; New roles of social partners in Europe* (pp. 21-37). Copenhagen: Copenhagen Centre.

Kyle, C. & Kantowicz, E. (1992). *Kids first-primero los niños.* Springfield: Illinois Issues.

Lagemann, E. (1989). *The politics of knowledge: The Carnegie Corporation, philanthropy and public policy.* Chicago: University of Chicago Press.

Lamb, R. (2002). Community support for music: Symphony education partnership. In Mitchell, S. *Effective educational partnerships* (pp. 137-155). Westport, CT: Preger.

Larson, G. (1997). *American canvas.* Washington, D. C. National Endowment for the Arts.

Lawton, M. (1997, September 17). Parents in N. Y. district to critique teachers. *Education Week*[On-line]. Available: http://www.EdWeek.com/h17.

Leadership Calgary (2002a). *Leadership Calgary* [On-line]. Available: http://www/volunteercalgary.ab.ca/LeadershipCalgary.

Leadership Calgary (2002b). *Highlights of the year.* Calgary: Leadership Calgary.

Leadership Ottawa (n.d.). *Leadership Ottawa: About us* [On-line]. Available: http://www.leadershipottawa. org/en/about_history.htm.

Legemann, E. (Ed.) (1999). *Philanthropic foundations: New scholarship new possibilities.* Bloomington, IN: Indiana University Press.

Lerman, R. (1996). Helping disconnected youth by improving linkages between high schools and careers. Paper prepared for the American Enterprise Institute Forum on America's Disconnected Youth [On-line]. Available: http://www.urban. org/pubs/disconec.htm.

Lewis, D. (1991, Feburary 18). Society and schools: The team system. *Washington*

Post.

Lewis, D. & Nakagawa, K.(1995).*A study of school decentralization.* Albany, NY:State University of New York.

Lightfoot, S. (1978). *Worlds apart: Relationships between families and schools.* New York: Basic Book.

Luellman, D. (2000, June). Public private partnerships: Selling off the future of public education. *Labour News* (Alberta Federation of Labour) [On-line]. Available:http://www.telusplanet.net/public/afl/LabourNews/june00-14-html.

McConnell (J. W.) Family Foundation (2002). *Community Leadership* [On-line]. Available: wysiwyg://69/http://www.mcconnellfoundation.ca/initiative.e/ community. html.

McCormick, M. & Wolf, J. (1993). Intervention Programs for Gifted Girls. *Roeper Review,* 16(2), 85-87.

McGivney, J. & Haught, J. (1972). The politics of education: A view from the perspective of the central office staff. *Educational Administration Quartley,* 8, 18-38.

McGrory, B. (1997, April 28). A new call to action: Political heavyweights gather to urge a spirit of volunteerism. *Boston Globe* [On line]. Available: http://www.boston.com/globe/htbin.

McKersie, W. (1993). Philanthropy's paradox: Chicago school reform, *Educational Evaluation and Policy Analysis,* 15(22), 109-128.

McKersie, W. (1999). Local philanthropy matter. In Lagemann, E. (Ed.). *Philanthropic Foundartions: New scholarship new possibilities* (pp. 329-358). Bloomington, IN: Indiana University Press.

Meyers, E. & McIssac, P. (Eds.) (1994). *How teachers are changing schools.* New York: IMPACT II-The Teachers Network.

Mezzacappa, D. (1997, April 23). Community service joins the syllabus in the region Students volunteering/ It's a matter of course. *The Philadelphia Inquirer*[On-line]. Available: http://www2.phillynews.com:80/ inquirer/html.

Michael, B. (1990). *Volunteers in public schools.* Washington,D.C.: National Academy Press.

Mikhailova, L. (2004). Council on International Educational Exchange. In Mitchell, S., Klinck, P., & Burger, J.(Eds.). *Worldwide partnerships for schools with voluntary organizations, foundations, universities, companies, and community councils* (pp. 89-122). Lewiston, NY: Edwin Mellen.

Mitchell, S. (1971). *A woman's profession, a man's research.* Edmonton, AB: Alberta Association of Registered Nurses.

Mitchell, S. (1990). *Innovation and reform.* York, ON: Captus.

Mitchell. S. (1995). *Sociology of educating.* York, ON: Captus.

Mitchell, S. (1996). *Tidal waves of school reform.* Westport, CT: Praeger.

Mitchell, S. (1998). *Reforming educators: Teachers, experts, and advocates.* Westport, CT: Praeger.

Mitchell, S. (2000a). *Partnerships in creative activities among schools, artists, and professional organizations.* Lewiston, NY.: Edwin Mellen.

Mitchell, S. (2000b). Rural Visions. Annual conference on Educational Access at the University of Arkansas at Pine Bluff, April 26, 2000.

Mitchell, S. (2001a). The Practice of Partnership. Paper delivered for Faculty of Education, Queens University.

Mitchell, S. (2001b). Partnerships and charter schools: Contrasts in Canadian Reform. *Encounters on Education.* Vol. 4, 91-103.

Mitchell, S. (2002) (Ed.). *Effective partnerships: Experts, advocates, and scouts.* Westport, CT: Praeger.

Mitchell, S. (2003). *The value of educational partnerships worldwide with the arts, science, business, and community organizations.* Lewiston, NY: Edwin Mellen.

Mitchell, S., Klinck, P., & Burger, J. (2004). *Worldwide partnerships for schools with voluntary organizations, foundations, universities, companies, and community councils.* Lewiston, N Y: Edwin Mellen.

Morgan, G. (1997). *Images of Organization.* Thousand Oaks, CA: Sage.

Mortensen, I. (2001, March). *First local report Hiiumaa, Estonia.* Copenhagen: Copenhagen Centre.

Mountain Institute (1998). Sacred mountains and environmental conservation: A practitioner's workshop. Spruce Knob Mountain Center, WV: Authors.

Moncey, D. & McQuillan, P. (1990). *Educational reform as revitalization movement.* Providence: The Coalition of Essential Schools.

Moyneux, P. & Wooley, M. (2004). Partnership for multigrade and bilingual education in Vietnam. In Mitchell, S., Klinck, P., & Burger, J. (Eds). *Worldwide partnerships for schools with voluntary organizations, foundations, universities, companies, and community councils (pp. 253-283).* Lewiston, NY: Edwin Mellen.

Murray-Seegert, C. (1989). *Nasty girls, thugs, and humans like us.* Baltimore: Paul Brookes.

National Alliance of Business (1991). *The Business Roundtable participation guide: A primer for business on education.* New York: Business Roundtable.

National Association for Music Education (n.d.). Oscar Mayer contest prize winners announced [On-line]. Available: wysiwyg://5/http://www.menc.org.

National Association of Partners in Education (2001). *Partnerships 2000: A decade of growth and change.* Alexandria, VA: National Association of Partners in Education.

National Commission on Civic Renewal (1998). *Final report of the National Commission on Civic Renewal* [On-line]. Available: http://www.puaf.umd.edu/ Affiliates/CivicR ...report.

National Commission on Service-Learning (2000). *Learning in deed* [On-line]. http://www.learningindeed.org/ tools/glance.html.

National Dropout Prevention Center Network (n.d.). *Mentoring overview* [On-line]. Available: http://www. dropoutprevention.org/effstrat/ment_tut/ment_over.html.

National Education Goals Panel. (1997, May 2). In the summit's wake: Volunteer activity. *Daily Report Card* [On-line]. Available: http;;www.utopia.com/mailings/

reportcard/html#index4.

Nelson, J. & Zadek, S. (2000). *Partnership alchemy: New social partnerships in Europe.* Copenhagen: Copenhagen Centre.

Noble, D. (2001). *Digital diploma mills: The automation of Higher Education.* New York: Monthly Review Press.

North Carolina Council of Churches (2002). Partnerships between schools and religious communities [On-line]. Available: http://www.nccouncilof churches. org/Sabbath/ Partnerships.html

Northeastern Illinois University (1994). *Breaking the invisible wall* (video). Chicago: Northeastern Illinois University Video Documentation Fund.

North West Regional Educational Laboratory (2001). *Accelerated Schools k-8* [On-line]. Available wysiwyg://16http://www.nwrel.org/scpd/catalog/ Model Details. asp?ModelID=1.

Office of National Drug Control Policy (2001, July). National youth anti-drug media campaign; multicultural outreach [On-line]. Available: http://www.media campaign.org/newsroom/080299/updatge8.html.

O'Connell, B. (1997). *Powered by coalition.* San Francisco: Jossey-Bass.

Office of Educational Research and Improvement, U. S. Department of Education (1992). Parental satisfaction with schools and the need for standards [On-line]. Available: http://www.ed.gov/pubs/OR/ ResearchRpts/parents.html.

Olson, L. (1984, November 7). 104 math and science teachers receive presidential accolade. *Education Week* [On-line]. Available: wysiwyg://24;;http://Edweek. org/ew/newstor.

Olson, L. (1997). *The school to work revolution.* Reading, MA: Addison-Wesley.

Olson, L. (2002). Critical voices. *Education Week, 22(02),* 28-31.

O'Neill, M. & Valenzuela, I. (1992). Michele Clark Middle School and the Algebra Project. *Reform Report, 2(8),* 5-8, 1.

Opinion Research Centre (1995). *Program evaluation of the mentoring program.* Dundas, Ontario: Big Brother Association of Burlington and Hamilton-Wentworth, Ontario.

Osborne, D. & Gaebler, T. (1992). *Reinventing government.* Reading: Addison-Westley.

Oxfam (n.d.). *Education now* [On-line]. Available: http://www.can.org.au/ oxfam/advocacy/education/report/chater6-2.html.

Pal, L. (2001). *Beyond policy analysis.* Scarborough, ON: Nelson Thompson Learning.

Pelz, D. (1957). *Motivation of the engineering and research specialist.* New York: American Management Association.

Perrin, S., & Oddleifson, E. (1996). *The power of the arts in education.* Nattick, Massachusetts: Center for Arts and Learning at Walnut Hill School and Hingham, Massachusetts: The Center for Arts in the Basic Curriculum.

Pew Charitable Trust (2001). Religion program overview [On-line]. Available: http://www.pewtrust.com/grants_ item.cfm?image=img 3&program_area_id=7.

Pollack, M. (2002). Student service in a nation's capital: Neighbors Project. In Mitchell, S. (Ed.) *Effective educational partnerships* (pp. 121-135). Westport, CT: Praeger.

Preparing North Carolina for 21st Century Schools (2000). *Programs leading North Carolina's preparation for 21st Century Schools* [On-line]. Available: http://www.ga. unc.edu/21stcentury schools/programs.

Reid, K. (2002, March 27). Aid plan launched for urban Christian schools. *Education* Week, 212(28), p. 5.

Rezin Orr Community Academy (n.d.). *Museum in the Classroom Project* [On-line]. Available: http:www.caa-archeology.org/~caamicp/orr/orrspash.htm.

Rigney, P. (2001). *Social dialogue and lifelong learning in Ireland* [On-line]. Available: www.etfr.eu.int/ letfwnnsfl/pages/downloadmalmo.2001.

Rizvi, S. & Sayee, A. (2004). Educational partnerships in northern Pakistan. In Mitchell, S., Klinck, P. , & Burger, J. (Eds.) *Worldwide partnerships for schools with voluntary organizations, foundations, univerities, companies, and community councils* (pp. 159-187). Lewiston, NY: Edwin Mellen.

Robinson, M. (1998). A collaboration model for school and community music education. *Arts Policy Review*, 100(2), 32-39.

Rud, A. & Oldendorf, W. (1992). *A place for teacher renewal.* New York: Teachers College.

Ryan, J., & Sakrey, C. (1984). *Strangers in paradise academics from the working class.* Boston: South End Press.

Save the Children (2002). Girls education: Strong beginnings [On-line]. Available: http://www. savethechildren.org/girlseducation/conclusion.shtml.

Sarason, S., & Lorentz, E. (1998). *Crossing boundaries: Collaboration, coordination, and the redefinition of resources.* San Francisco: Jossey-Bass.

Science Alberta Partnership (2002). Regional Science Networks [On-line]. Available: http://www.sciencealberta.org.

Sansbury, J. (2004, January 23). Dekalb schools pair with colleges. *Atlanta Journal-Constitution [On-line]. Available: http://www.ajc.com/friday/content/epaper/ editions/fridaymetro 04013cOcf3d9612d81000.h....*

Shaw. G. (2002). *Ethnic minority employment through partnerships.* Copenhagen: Copenhagen Centre.

Short, C. (1998). The Cultural Metamorphosis of Cree Education. M. A. Thesis. University of Calgary.

Southest Center for Teacher Quality (2002). *Thinking out of the box* [On-line]. Available: http://www. teachingquality.org.

Shumer, R. (1999). *The status of service-Learning in the United States* [On-line]. Available: http://www. service-learning.org/library/online-documents/status.html.

Sironek, K. & Goodlad, J. (1988). *School-university partnerships in action.* New York: Teachers College, Columbia University.

Smith, L., Klein, P., Prunty, J., & Dwyer, D. (1986). *Educational innovators: Then and now.* London: The Falmer Press.

Sommerfeld, M. (1994, January 12). Annenberg gift prompts praise and questions. *Education Week*, 13(16), 1,12.

Stainburn, S. (2002, August). It don't mean a thing if it ain't got that swing. *Teacher Magazine, 14(01), 22-27*.

Stake, R., Bresler, L., & Mabry, L. (1991). *Custom & cherishing: The arts in elementary schools*. Urbana, Il: National Arts Education Research Center, University of Illinois.

Stacey, E. & Wiesenberg, F. (2004). An on-line cross-global educational project. In Mitchell, S., Klinck, P., & Burger, J. (Eds.). *Worldwide partnerships for schools with voluntary organizations, foundations, universities, companies, and community councils* (pp. 65-86). Lewiston, NY: Edwin Mellen.

Steele, U. & Boyle, P. (1997). Systemic approaches to systemic discrimination. Unpublished paper.

Stuts, T. (2000, February 4). Study links school size, test scores; Smaller campuses aid lower-income youths. *Dallas News*. URL: http://dallasnews.com.

Strom, R. & Strom, S. (1995). Intergenerational learning:Grandparents in the schools. *Educational Gerontology*, 21(4), 321-335.

Tennessee Department of Education (n.d.). *Three Statewide Programs in Arts Education ACT III Arts Consortium of Tennessee*. Nashville, TN: Tennessee Department of Education.

Thompson, J. (1967). *Organizations in action*. New York: McGraw-Hill.

Thompson, M. (1999). The 'science'' and 'art' of teaching and learning at Xavier University of Louisiana. In Foster, L., Guyden, J., & Miller, A. (Eds). *Affirmed action* (pp. 51-60). Landam, Maryland: Rowman & Littlefield.

Tourse, R. & Mooney, J. (1999). *Collaborative Practice*. Westport, CT: Praeger.

Trottner, A. (1997, April 23). Parents, educators make new connection with the internet. *Education Week* [On-line]. Available: http://www.EdWeek.com/htbin.

United States Agency for International Development, Office of Women in Development (n.d.). *Educational partnerships for girls: Development success* [On-line]. Available: http://www.usaid.gov/wid/pubs/ib2.html.

United States Department of Education, Office of Educational Research and Improvement (1996). *Educational partnerships case studies*. Washington, D. C.: U. S. Office of Education.

Viadero, D. (2002). Study shows test gains in 'Accelerated Schools.' *Education Week*, 21(16), 6.

Vestergaard, M. (2001). *First local report Limerick, Ireland*. Copenhagen: Copenhagen Centre.

Washburn, G. & Martinez, M. (1997, Septmber 4). Chicago's schools add s to 3 r's high school students will have to do service. *Chicago Tribune*. [On-line]. Available: http://www.chicagotribune.com.html.

Weisman, J. (1990, October 24). Macy to expand accelerated program for minorities. *Education Week*. Available: http://EdWeek.org/ew/ewstory.cfm?slug =10390031.h10.

Weisman, J. (1991, July 31). PTA principals on corporate support fail to win over other organizations. *Education Week*. [On-line]. Available: http://www.EdWeek. com/htbin.

Weissman, D. (1993, November). Group aim to put street gangs on better path. *Catalyst*, 5(3),6.

Wheeler, A. & Pardham, S. (2004). Cross-cultural learning in a teacher education. In Mitchell, S., Klink, P., & Burger, J. (Eds.) *Worldwide partnerships for schools with voluntary organizations, foundations, universities, companies, and community councils* (pp. 123-157). Lewiston, NY: Edwin Mellen.

Whitty, G., Power, S., & Haplin, D. (1998). *Devolution & choice in education*. Bristol, PA: Open University Press.

Williams, E. & August, B. (1994). Learning from Success: Strategies and Implications. In Berne, R. & Picus, L. (Eds). *Outcome equity in education (pp. 87-105)*. Thousand Oaks, CA: Corwin Press.

Women's Learning Partnership (2000-2003). *About us* [On-line]. Available: http://www.learningpartnership. org/about/index.html.

Yankelovich, D. (1991). *Coming to public judgment*. Syracuse, N. Y.: Syracuse University Press.

Zadek, S., Hojensgard, N., & Raynard, P. (2001). *Perspectives on the new economy of corporate citizenship*. Copenhagen: Copenhagen Centre.

Index

170

Education, 46.
National Science Foundation, 20
New York City, 18. 24- 25, 34, 35,
38, 60
Neighbors Project, 26-28, 30
North Carolina, 58, 87, 95, 108, 117-
120
North Carolina Center for the
Advancement of Teaching
(NCATT), 117-120, 122 131
Organizational theory, 57-58, 76
Organic intellectuals, 105-108
Orr Network, 98-102
Pakistan, 62, 96-98, 138
Parents, 3, 4, 60, 64 -67, 70-73, 94
Parent Teachers Association, 9, 65
Prevention Las Vegas (PAL), 17
Public/private cooperation, 11, 79,
136- 138, 146
Religion, 6-7, 10, 79, 85-90, 105,
146, 153
Retirees, 4, 9, 67-68, 70, 76
Rochester Eastman School String
Partnership (RESP), 18-19, 34
r.u.mad? 146-149
School-to-work, 25, 30-32, 42, 71
Science, 15, 22-25, 35-36, 42, 79
Social indicators, 11, 123-127, 132-
133
Social movement, 10, 79-109
South Carolina, 22, 56, 93, 145
Student leaders, 50-52, 82, 107-109
St. Xavier, Francis, University, 23
Tennessee, 52-54, 56, 72, 75
Ventures in Education (VIE), 24, 39-
40, 133
Vietnam, 106-108
Visions, 1, 10, 55-57, 77
Volunteers, 26, 28-29, 30, 37, 45-50,
52, 60-61, 64-67, 69-71, 73, 76, 91-
92, 133, 138, 139, 145-146
Universities, 37,95-97, 100, 137 143
Triangle Coalition, 22-23

Women, 2, 5, 12, 107-108, 112, 127-
132, 134, 143

MELLEN STUDIES IN EDUCATION

27. Xiufeng Liu, **Mathematics and Science Curriculum Change in the People's Republic of China**

28. Judith Evans Longacre, **The History of Wilson College 1868 to 1970**

29. Thomas E. Jordan, **The First Decade of Life, Volume I: Birth to Age Five**

30. Thomas E. Jordan, **The First Decade of Life, Volume II: The Child From Five to Ten Years**

31. Mary I. Fuller and Anthony J. Rosie (eds.), **Teacher Education and School Partnerships**

32. James J. Van Patten (ed.), **Watersheds in Higher Education**

33. K. (Moti) Gokulsing and Cornel DaCosta (eds.), **Usable Knowledges as the Goal of University Education: Innovations in the Academic Enterprise Culture**

34. Georges Duquette (ed.), **Classroom Methods and Strategies for Teaching at the Secondary Level**

35. Linda A. Jackson and Michael Murray, **What Students Really Think of Professors: An Analysis of Classroom Evaluation Forms at an American University**

36. Donald H. Parkerson and Jo Ann Parkerson, **The Emergence of the Common School in the U.S. Countryside**

37. Neil R. Fenske, **A History of American Public High Schools, 1890-1990: Through the Eyes of Principals**

38. Gwendolyn M. Duhon Boudreaux (ed.), **An Interdisciplinary Approach to Issues and Practices in Teacher Education**

39. John Roach, **A Regional Study of Yorkshire Schools 1500-1820**

40. V.J. Thacker, **Using Co-operative Inquiry to Raise Awareness of the Leadership and Organizational Culture in an English Primary School**

41. Elizabeth Monk-Turner, **Community College Education and Its Impact on Socioeconomic Status Attainment**

42. George A: Churukian and Corey R. Lock (eds.), **International Narratives on Becoming a Teacher Educator: Pathways to a Profession**

43. Cecilia G. Manrique and Gabriel G. Manrique, **The Multicultural or Immigrant Faculty in American Society**

44. James J. Van Patten (ed.), **Challenges and Opportunities for Education in the 21st Century**

45. Barry W. Birnbaum, **Connecting Special Education and Technology for the 21st Century**

46. J. David Knottnerus and Frédérique Van de Poel-Knottnerus, **The Social Worlds of Male and Female Children in the Nineteenth Century French Educational System: Youth, Rituals, and Elites**

47. Sandra Frey Stegman, **Student Teaching in the Choral Classroom: An Investigation of Secondary Choral Music Student Teachers' Perceptions of Instructional Successes and Problems as They Reflect on Their Music Teaching**

48. Gwendolyn M. Duhon and Tony Manson (eds.), **Preparation, Collaboration, and Emphasis on the Family in School Counseling for the New Millennium**

49. Katherina Danko-McGhee, **The Aesthetic Preferences of Young Children**

50. Jane Davis-Seaver, **Critical Thinking in Young Children**

51. Gwendolyn M. Duhon and Tony J. Manson (eds.), **Implications for Teacher Education – Cross-Ethnic and Cross-Racial Dynamics of Instruction**

52. Samuel Mitchell, **Partnerships in Creative Activities Among Schools, Artists and Professional Organizations Promoting Arts Education**

53. Loretta Niebur, **Incorporating Assessment and the National Standards for Music Education into Everyday Teaching**